THE M-FILES

True Reports of Minnesota's Unexplained Phenomena

by jay rath

Wisconsin Trails
Madison, Wisconsin

17.95

First edition, first printing
Copyright © 1998 Jay Rath

Library of Congress Catalog Card Number: 98-61219
ISBN: 0-915024-66-7

Editors: Elizabeth McBride & Chris Roerden
Cover Design: Kathie Campbell
Designer: Denise Knudsvig
Illustrations: Jay Rath

Printed in the United States of America by McNaughton & Gunn, Inc.

This book was not approved, prepared, licensed or endorsed
by any entity involved in creating or producing "The X-Files."

Alpine

Wisconsin Tales and Trails
P.O. Box 5650
Madison, WI 53705
(800) 236-8088
E-mail: info@wistrails.com

June, 1999

For Kevin, Lon, Gordon, Cletus, Shana and Judy,
and all the other friends I made in Center City, Minn.

TABLE OF CONTENTS

Acknowledgments vii

Introduction ix

Invitation to Readers. xiii

Partial Bibliography xiv

The Ice Man Cometh 1

Alien in a Can. 8

Bigfoot 13

The Giant Bunnies of Lake Wobegon. 22

UFOs Before There Were UFOs 25

Land of 10,000 Flying Saucers. 34

The Astronaut's UFO 52

Cereal Saucers. 55

Blackout! 59

When Prophecy Comes True 62

Trail of the Vikings 85

Cattle Mutilations. 99

Fairies and Sun Dogs 109

Place-Name Index. 115

ACKNOWLEDGMENTS

Richard Heiden has been enormously helpful to me in my UFO research, and I cannot overemphasize the value of his contributions. I'm also especially indebted to Loren Coleman, one of America's leading investigators of unexplained phenomena. I would also like to thank Andy Hager, who made the completion of the manuscript possible.

INTRODUCTION

"If we lose a sense of the mysterious,
life is no more than a snuffed out candle."
—Albert Einstein

What is truth—something we believe or something we know? I think it's a two-step process, with belief first and knowledge second. Here's an experiment you can run in your own mind. Let's take an actual report of a UFO:

A man and a woman are on a train. They look out over the countryside and see a UFO. The man recalls later that the UFO must have been 800 feet long. He says, "While we were watching the cigar-shaped thing for four or five minutes as it paced the train, we noticed that another object had joined it. The second object appeared very suddenly in back of the first one. It was a disc-shaped thing. Both of them were very shiny.

"If my estimate of size on the cigar-shaped thing was correct, then the disc-shaped object would have been about 100 feet in diameter, flat on the bottom with a shallow dome on top. My wife and I watched them for another two or three minutes. They were moving at about the same speed as the train and they were very close to the top of the ridge, not more than 500 feet above it, I would say. Then they began to rise, slowly at first and then much faster. In a matter of seconds they had risen so high that we couldn't see them anymore from the train window."

Let's begin our experiment. There is a big gap between believing that flying saucers are real, for example, and *knowing* that they are real. If we are satisfied with a person's UFO report, if we are satisfied that they know what they're talking about—if we *believe* in the witness—then we can know that the UFO is real. So to decide something is "really" true—to know it—we have to develop unscientific faith, usually in the witness. In developing that faith we must overcome an internal prejudice linked to proximity.

In your mind, you must already have an idea of how "true" you think the above report is. I will make the report "truer" to you. The man was the curator of an astronomical observatory.

You now have greater faith in the witness, don't you? What if I told you that the sighting was made in Minnesota? You have even greater faith in the truth of the sighting.

Next I will take away some of that faith: it didn't happen in Minnesota, but 100 miles west of Las Vegas. You probably believe a little less now. But I'll push your faith way up again by giving you the name of the witness and the date, and especially by returning the Minnesota tie: the sighting was made on Nov. 1, 1955, by Frank Halstead, former curator of the University of Minnesota's Darling Observatory in Duluth.

There is a lesson here, and I think it is very interesting. The lesson is that we are not naturally gullible UFO believers. We have a sense of our local environments based on our own experiences, and we therefore trust them more. Deep down, I guess, we are suspicious of strangers, and even of the state of reality in lands far away. A UFO in Minnesota is more real to Minnesotans than a UFO in Nevada.

That's the main reason I wrote this book. There are a lot of excellent reports of various phenomena around the world, but they just won't count as much as reports from our neighborhood. Another reason for collecting an individual state's unexplained phenomena was outlined in one of the few truly classic works in the field of "ufology," John Fuller's *Incident at Exeter.* Fuller examined a wave of UFO reports centered at Exeter, N.H., and suggested that the microcosm might provide answers that the macrocosm could not.

He wrote, "If the reports in a concentrated area turned out to show many similarities, perhaps some conclusions could be drawn about the possible patterns of the objects, not readily evident from widely scattered reports."

Besides their possible scientific and entertainment value, these stories are valuable for what they tell us about ourselves. So said Prof. Robert A. Brightman, a cultural anthropologist, when I interviewed him at the University of Wisconsin-Madison.

Brightman investigated Bigfoot sightings, not because he wanted to prove whether or not the creature exists. In fact, he believed it does not. His interest was in why people *wanted* to believe the stories. Brightman wasn't scrutinizing Bigfoot. He was scrutinizing us.

"I think it fits into a larger tendency that you can observe in every human society," he said. "Images like Bigfoot—images between humans and animals—seem to be common to people of all states of society. If it's not universal, it's close to universal."

History contains many stories of half-human, half-animal monsters, such as the centaur, the minotaur and the mermaid. And today there is Nepal's Yeti, or Abominable Snowman. In Russia they call a similar creature Omah. In China it is the Wildman. On our continent the legend of the Yeti is termed Bigfoot, and it varies regionally, each with a local name: Sasquatch, Bushman, Creek Devil, Big Mo, Smya Likh, Mountain Devil and Dsonqua. Minnesota's Native Americans called it Windigo.

It could be that each of these peoples invents Bigfoot and other monsters because the inventions serve a purpose. Prof. Brightman talked of it as our need to psychologically separate our culture from nature, to know how we are different. Reports of Bigfoot, for example, fill the bill in three ways:

First, there is Bigfoot the Monster. Under this heading fall the stories of a huge, slavering creature that stalks humans and attempts to kill and eat them. This Bigfoot is in the classical tradition of the wild man and werewolf.

Second, there is Bigfoot the House Pet, a docile, dependent creature in need of human aid. (An example of this is the story of an Alberta, Canada, farm girl who discovered a female Sasquatch in labor inside the family barn. The girl assisted in the delivery. In the dawn, the creature left.

Third, there is Bigfoot, Friend of Man. In this category are the tales of injured hunters and travelers befriended by the gentle giants, who aid them. Sometimes the creatures lead the humans to a cave or dwelling where Bigfoot families are observed, complete with speech and teenagers.

In all of these stories human qualities are contrasted with those of a beast, an animal we call Bigfoot. It is wild; we are civilized. It is helpless; we are skilled. It is subservient; we are dominant.

The exercise and the lessons it teaches are clear. The more closely the creature resembles us, the more specific we can make the rules for membership in the human club. We are not animals, we are not monsters—we are not Bigfoot.

Other phenomena, real or not, undeniably serve similar emotional needs. It is interesting to note, for example, that although strange objects have been seen in the skies since Biblical times, it has only been since 1947 that UFOs were thought to be spacecraft. Before that, they were "mystery airships," perhaps dirigibles. Earlier UFOs were signs from God.

I don't want the reader to think that unexplained phenomena are to be studied only as folklore. Some Minnesota unexplained phenomena are too real. For example, in August 1995 elementary schoolchildren at Henderson studied a farm pond 55 miles southwest of Minneapolis and found 200 frogs with multiple, missing or twisted legs. Some of the frogs had abnormal eyes. By 1996, scientists in 54 of Minnesota's 87 counties had found similar frog mutations. They were also found in Oregon, Vermont, Wisconsin and Quebec, Canada.

What causes such phenomena? The list of suspects includes global warming, parasites, acid rain, water pollution, and the thinning ozone layer. No one yet knows why the deformities occur. The fear, of course, is that whatever is happening will start to climb the evolutionary ladder, affecting more complex organisms, such as people who buy books on unexplained phenomena.

The reader's response may be, "Well, the frog mutations are completely different from UFO stories because the mutations are real. This is a very serious matter, and to mention it in a book on flying saucers and things like that is a bit offensive."

To be honest, that's the response I want, because I hope it will lead the reader to meditate on just why the frog mutations are more "real" than the other stories in this book. Again, what is the difference between believing something and knowing something?

We go on from here to deal with stories that are whimsical, some that are outrageous, and some that are truly alarming. From mutated frogs to mutilated cattle, from UFOs to Bigfoot and fairies—all deserve our attention and respect. In any of these fields of investigation, I think it's best to remember the words of the UFO witness we cited above, Frank Halstead, the former curator of the University of Minnesota's Darling Observatory.

"Credible witnesses all over the world are reporting incidents similar to mine," he said. "It does not alter the existing facts if these people are held up to ridicule. The time is long overdue for accepting the presence of these things, whatever they are, and dealing with them—and the public—on a basis of reality and honesty."

An Invitation

If you have stories about unexplained phenomena in Wisconsin, Iowa, Minnesota, Michigan or Illinois, please share them with me. I can be reached in care of Wisconsin Trails, P.O. Box 5650, Madison, WI 53705.

Partial Bibliography

The material for this book came from a variety of sources, including personal interviews, U.S. Air Force files, and newspapers, especially the St. Paul *Pioneer Press*. Other printed sources include:

Blegen, Theodore C. *The Kensington Runestone: New Light on an Old Riddle.* St. Paul: Minnesota Historical Society, 1968.

Blum, Howard. *Out There.* New York: Simon & Schuster, 1990.

Bowen, Charles, ed. *The Humanoids.* Chicago: Henry Regnery Co., 1969.

Bryan, C.D.B. *Close Encounters of the Fourth Kind: Alien Abduction, UFOs and the Conference at M.I.T.* New York: Alfred A. Knopf, 1995.

Byrne, Peter. *The Search for Bigfoot: Monster, Myth or Man?* New York: Pocket Books, 1976.

Cohen, Daniel. *The Great Airship Mystery: A UFO of the 1890's.* New York: Dodd, Mead & Co., 1981.

Coleman, Loren. *Mysterious America.* Boston: Faber and Faber, 1983.

Condon, Dr. Edward U. *Final Report of the Scientific Study of Unidentified Flying Objects.* Washington, D.C.: U.S. Dept. of Commerce, 1968.

Corliss, William. *Handbook of Unusual Natural Phenomena.* Garden City, N.Y.: Anchor Press/Doubleday, 1983.

Doyle, Arthur Conan. *The History of Spiritualism.* New York: Arno Press, 1975 (reprint).

Fawcett, Lawrence, and Greenwood, Barry J. *Clear Intent: The Government Cover-up of the UFO Experience.* Englewood Cliffs, N.J.: PrenticeHall, 1984.

Festinger, Leon; Riecken, Henry W.; and Schachter, Stanley. *When Prophecy Fails.* Minneapolis: University of Minnesota Press, 1956.

Gilman, Rhoda, ed. *A Yankee Inventor's Flying Ship.* St. Paul: Minnesota Historical Society, 1969.

Gourley, Jay. *The Great Lakes Triangle.* Greenwich, Conn.: Fawcett, 1977.

Green, Gabriel. *Let's Face the Facts About Flying Saucers.* New York:

Popular Library, 1967.

Green, John. *The Sasquatch File.* Agassiz, British Columbia: Cheam Publishing Ltd., 1973.

Hall, Richard, ed. *The UFO Evidence.* Washington, D.C.: National Investigations Committee on Aerial Phenomena, 1964.

Holand, Hjalmar R. *A Pre-Columbian Crusade to America.* New York: Twayne Publishers, 1962.

Hynek, J. Allen. *The Hynek UFO Report.* New York: Dell Publishing, 1977.

Jones, Rev. Peter. *History of the Ojibway Indians* (sic). London: A.W. Bennett, 1861.

Kohl, Johann Georg. *Kitchi-Gami: Life Among the Lake Superior Ojibway* (sic). Minneapolis: Minnesota Historical Society Press, 1985 (reprint).

Lansberg, Alan. *In Search of ...* New York: Everest House, 1978.

Leslie, Desmond, and Adamski, George. *Flying Saucers Have Landed.* London: Werner Laurie, 1953.

Marrs, Jim. *Alien Agenda: Investigating the Extraterrestrial.* New York: HarperCollins, 1997.

Napier, John Russell. *Bigfoot.* New York: Berkley Medallion Books, 1972.

Olsen, Thomas M. *The Reference for Outstanding UFO Reports.* Riderwood, Md.: UFO Information Retrieval Center, Inc., 1966.

Ruppelt, Edward J. *The Report on Unidentified Flying Objects.* Garden City, NY: Doubleday & Co., 1956.

Shackley, Myra. *Still Living? Yeti, Sasquatch and the Neanderthal Enigma.* New York: Thames and Hudson, 1983.

Vallee, Jacques. *Passport to Magonia: From Folklore to Flying Saucers.* Chicago: Henry Regnery Co., 1969.

Winchell, N.H. ed. *The Aborigines of Minnesota.* St. Paul: The Pioneer Company, 1911. Mead & Co., 1981.

THE ICE MAN COMETH

"I was raped by the Abominable Snowman," read the headline in *The National Journal*, and it didn't happen on Mt. Everest, the Snowman's traditional habitat. It happened in Minnesota—if it happened at all.

Even if it did, it didn't happen that way, as it wasn't the Abominable Snowman but Bigfoot, a distinction that would hardly have mattered to the poor victim, of course, but we're trying to be scientific. The account was one of several stories explaining a carcass, found frozen in a block of ice, of a Bigfoot-type creature that turned up in the Gopher state. It was called Ice Man, and it was examined by scientists—even by the Smithsonian Institution. Some pronounced it real. Some did not.

There were three stories explaining the body's origin, the most improbable being the sexual assault tale. The woman involved, Helen Westring, said she was hunting alone near Bemidji when the incident occurred. She seems to have been carrying a rifle, not a shotgun, so she must have been hunting deer. It would have been a better story if she hadn't been hunting at all, and was therefore more of an innocent, but that would be embroidering the truth, and of course this report attempts to be factual; though why she would be hunting deer alone is unusual. Any game big enough to hit with a rifle is something a hunter would want help in dragging out of the woods.

Anyway, she had a gun. She encountered a huge furry creature on two legs. It had pink eyes and brown hair, she told *The National Journal*, one of our finer supermarket newspapers, in its June 30, 1969, issue. The beast quickly grabbed her and ripped off her clothes, "like one would peel a banana," Westring said. After Westring had been peeled, the beast, she said, stared at "the area between my legs." The creature threw her down, and Ms. Westring fortunately fainted before she was, as she claimed, sexually assaulted. Upon regaining consciousness, she grabbed her rifle and shot the beast through its right eye.

She chose a head shot, especially the eye, because it would almost certainly ensure the quickest death. If she had been shooting a deer, she would have done the same to save the meat, but we can probably set this possibility aside. No, she went for the eye because it was fast and, of course, poetic. You or I probably wouldn't especially care where we shot it, and would have shot it in the chest, or even the ear, or most especially the groin, which to tabloid readers would be almost as poetic. But she shot it in the eye and her innocence was avenged—artistically. She apparently then recovered the carcass, so that Frank Hansen of Winona could exhibit it at carnivals.

Ms. Westring's little wooden sled of a story creaks under the weight of the Ice Man. Fortunately, we have another, more robust, story: Frank Hansen was on a hunting trip to Bemidji in 1961 with some other Air Force personnel and became separated from his party. He shot a doe, and it fled, wounded. Tracking it, he found his prey in a swamp, where three hairy, upright creatures were tearing it apart with their hands and drinking its blood. One of the beasts sprang at Hansen, and the hunter was just seconds from being killed or having his clothes peeled before he shot the monster very poetically through its right eye, killing it instantly. Hansen fled, and kept his story secret from his companions.

But the truth gnawed at him; the creature had been so human— had he committed murder? He returned later and found the body intact, frozen solid in the Minnesota December. To leave the body was to invite detection, possibly prosecution for murder! Better to haul the evidence off. But how could he possibly drag the huge, stiff carcass away by himself without at least chopping it into luggage-sized pieces? Hansen always left this part of the story out.

Nevertheless, he brought the Ice Man out whole, brought the body to his Air Force quarters and hid it in his large freezer. We must assume that he bundled the furry stiff pretty well, to avoid comment by the sentries at the Air Force base gate. We must also assume that his Air Force neighbors did not take an interest in the bundle as he hefted it inside his house. Keep in mind that Hansen later claimed he took all these actions to avoid the suspicion that he had committed murder. To achieve this transport, he must have carefully planned it in advance, deciding that leaving Ice Man dead in the woods was not nearly so suspicious as bringing him whole into the busy and populous air base. We must therefore assume that he believed such behavior would be overlooked at an Air Force base.

Upon arriving home, he surprised his wife with the news that he had brought somebody home with him. Mrs. Hansen agreeably threw out all the regular frozen groceries from their spacious freezer. For seven years the two kept their guest on ice, hidden from the eyes of all.

This story is also a bit difficult to believe. Fortunately we have yet a third version to consider: the creature was not from Minnesota at all. It was reportedly found, already frozen, in a 6,000-pound block of ice floating in the Sea of Okhotsk, near eastern Siberia. It was found by Russian seal hunters or—in yet another version of the story—by Japanese whalers. They smuggled it to Hong Kong, where it was bought by an American millionaire who lived on the West Coast. He in turn rented the curiosity to Air Force veteran Frank Hansen of Winona, who then exhibited the find at fairs.

Of all the events in any of the above scenarios, only one thing is certain: Frank Hansen exhibited the creature at fairs. The next certainty is that his exhibit was spotted by Milwaukee zoologist Terry Cullen in December 1968 at Chicago's International Livestock Exhibition and Fair. Cullen called a civilian research group, the Society for the Investigation of the Unexplained, in New Jersey. The carnival pitch that Hansen was using at the time was the Japanese whaler version, which no one believed. Still, the body itself was interesting. The society's celebrated investigator and administrative director, scientist Ivan Sanderson, later wrote, "Mr. Cullen's report included some details of this corpse's appearance that, taken together, prompted us to

3

seriously consider the possibility of its being a real body, and not just a model ...."

Sanderson traveled to Hansen's farm near Winona to have a peek, and he took along a heavyweight zoologist and expert on early hominids, Dr. Bernard Huevelmans, of the Zoological Society of London. Though the carnival curious had to pay 35 cents for a few minutes with the Ice Man, Sanderson and Huevelmans studied it free for three days, beginning Dec. 16, 1968. They needed every minute; the view was poor.

By this time the creature had been encased in a block of ice that measured 6 feet 11 inches long, 2 feet 8 inches wide and 3 feet 6 inches deep. The creature itself was about 6 feet tall—short for Bigfoot. Sanderson wrote that "considerable sections of the ice have recrystallized in tabular plastrons of opaque construction." That means the ice was frosty.

"Second, there has been considerable exudation of gases from the corpse forced outward from all orifices and from skin pores through the hair-fine tubules that penetrate even clear, amorphous, palaeocrystic, and other forms of ice." That means there were bubbles in it.

The ice block sat inside an insulated coffin that measured 3 feet by 7 feet 4 inches, covered by four layers of plate glass. A foot in from each end, the block was strapped down by nylon straps. The whole affair was being carted around in a cramped trailer, and Sanderson and Huevelmans had to use strong floodlights and even lie on top of the ice to get a good look and make sketches. To make matters even more interesting, Sanderson quickly discovered that "the hair-fine tubules that penetrate even clear, amorphous, palaeocrystic, and other forms of ice" allow odors to escape.

"The corpse, or whatever it is, is rotting," he wrote. "This could be detected by a strong stench—typical of rotting mammalian flesh .... Whatever this corpse may be, it would seem to include flesh of some kind; and such cannot be preserved permanently in mere ice."

As you may have already gathered, Sanderson was death on details. If he could have counted the hairs, he would have. Let me condense his detailed findings:

The hair: It wasn't just fur stapled to a frame, or a collection of wigs. There were lots of hairs in some areas, just a few or none in others. If fake, the hairs would have to have been inserted individually. The hair was jet black and dark brown. Each individual hair seemed to have light and dark bands, a condition called "agouti," which is most definitely not found in hominids (us) or pongids (the great apes, etc.) but is found in our smaller cousins, the monkeys.

The face: Sanderson couldn't make out the shape of the head, but he did see the part closest to the surface of the ice, which fortunately for carnival-goers was the face. (Also a highlight was the penis, but you'll have to wait—more on this later.) The face was yellowish pink, like that of a human Caucasian. The forehead sloped only a little, not what you'd expect from a cave man or gorilla. The eyes were big, or would have been if they'd been there. Rather, the sockets were big. From the left socket came a stream of blood; remember that this was where, in other stories, the bullet entered. Ice Man also had a very wide pug nose.

The torso: Bulky, with wide shoulders, and tapering only slightly to the hips. "The nipples are rather far to the sides." No real neck.

The arms: The upper arms were thinner than the forearms—sort of a Popeye effect. The limbs had the longest hair on the whole body.

The hands: Large—larger than you'd expect, even given the creature's size. The thumb was fully opposed, like our own.

The genitalia: "Rather slender, and tapers to a point." No hair, though some on the scrotum. The penis was pale yellow.

The legs: Hard to see—the knees looked pretty human.

The feet: These are important parts for classification purposes. Sanderson observed them to be definitely human-like, and compared them favorably to fossilized tracks left by the Neanderthal, a broad, squat cousin of humankind who lived about 75,000 years ago. "The toes are astonishingly equal in size, the little-toe being large and the great-toe being rather small in proportion (compared to a human's). All form an almost straight 'front' which would seem to be the ideal conformation for steady forward progress in snow or loose soils." Behind the toes was a pad that extended all the way across the foot. (Sanderson did not consider it, but this feature precisely describes the manner in which Bigfoot tracks differ from the merely enlarged human footprints left by hoaxers. Bigfoot feet are not just big human feet. I don't want to go into more detail here for fear of giving hoaxers tips on better ways to leave false tracks. Suffice it to say that if the Ice Man had gotten up and taken a walk, he would have left tracks indistinguishable from the best, most trustworthy Bigfoot tracks found.)

In all, as Sanderson summarized, "This body is not that of any known hominid or pongid and, what is more significant, it does not conform to any reconstruction or artist's conception of any fossil man or ape or other anthropoid. Its general features and particular characteristics ... display an extraordinary mixture of what have until now been assigned either to men or apes," but never to both.

Sanderson and Huevelmans believed that what they observed was a form of Neanderthal man, and that therefore the Neanderthal race had survived until today, to become known as Bigfoot.

So was Ice Man real? "I personally agree that it was," stated another Bigfoot expert, Peter Byrne, a big game hunter who actually went out to hunt Bigfoot (with a camera) while others sat back and pontificated.

Others were less impressed—much less. Another celebrated Bigfoot advocate, primate biologist John Napier, was contacted by Sanderson and given the exhaustive report. Napier said that the Ice Man seemed "to combine the worst features of apes and man and none of the best features which make these two groups successful primates in their respective environments." He did concede that such unlikely combinations could and did occur in evolution, but pointed out that when they did, the in-between adaptations were well-suited to conditions on the globe at the time.

Huevelmans in February 1969 announced that he and Sanderson had found in the Ice Man proof of an unknown form of living hominid. He officially reported it in the *Bulletin of the Royal Institute of Natural Sciences of Belgium*. He even gave the creature a Latin name, *Homo pongoides*, so that it could be included right beside *Homo sapiens* (us) and *Homo erectus* (great, great, great, etc., grandpa). This was really jumping the gun as far as zoologists were concerned. Sanderson printed his own more-cautious report in the journal *Genus*.

There followed a lot of popular press attention. John Napier, then with the Smithsonian Institution, did some digging. He turned up a Hollywood company that claimed credit for making the Ice Man. Actually, in light of the attendant publicity, there were a total of three Hollywood companies claiming that honor. Count on Hollywood for the truth. But because of this, the Smithsonian issued a press release stating that it was withdrawing its interest—which in itself was newsworthy. Time-Life Inc. made a film. Huevelmans and Sanderson did more investigating. Meanwhile, the Ice Man had changed.

Frank Hansen said that the original Ice Man had been removed by its West Coast millionaire owner. In its place, at great expense, Hansen had substituted a man-made copy. Sanderson and Huevelmans looked at it and agreed that this was not the same creature they had previously viewed. Napier practically giggled, observing, "There is still no certainty that the 'original' was any more 'real' than the substituted model."

It was at this time that Hansen started changing his story—it was shot by a woman, it was shot by himself. Once the Ice Man appeared at carnivals, the FBI actually was consulted, and although they weren't taking any action at the moment, Hansen said he felt safer from prosecution with an admitted model on display. That part of his changing story I do believe.

Hansen apparently no longer resides in Winona, if he is even living. I have heard, however, that the substitute Ice Man still turns up at fairs.

Was it real? Is it still frozen somewhere, maybe in California, the private toy of an eccentric millionaire? I would think such a tale were impossible, but then Michael Jackson really did try to buy the bones of Britain's Elephant Man. What makes one wonder is that the thing stank so much. That most definitely would not have been an added attraction at fairs; almost all who saw it would have expected that ice and four pieces of plate glass would have preserved it perfectly, never stopping to think how odors travel to other foods from the frozen fish in their own freezers. Thus, no one would have found an odor to be added evidence. But there was an odor, and that suggests that Ice Man may have been real.

If I had to put a number to it, I'd say I am 80 percent certain that the Ice Man was a hoax. Maybe it's because it's too difficult for me to believe that someone could bring in the flesh of a Bigfoot.

As for bones—that's another matter. Minnesota has bones, lots of bones, of what could be Bigfoot. But that's a later chapter.

ALIEN IN A CAN

A liens become boring after awhile. There is such a sameness to it all, even down to the descriptions. The usual aliens divide up as: the "grays"—those short, sexless folk with the wrap-around eyes; the "Nordics"—pleasant, human-looking chaps with blue eyes, blonde hair and jumpsuits; and the "reptilians"—6 to 8 feet tall, four-clawed hand—nasty. Out of 203 cases describing alien encounters in the United States, according to a recent presentation on the alien abduction phenomena at the Massachusetts Institute of Technology, 137 were humanoid—that is, mostly the Nordics and grays: two legs, two arms, two eyes, one head, no tail.

Well, ho-hum. This sort of sameness is just one of the factors arguing in favor of the phenomenon's reality, of course—lots of people describing the same thing; it would be easier to write it all off if every witness had his or her own alien who had never been seen by anyone else. But after awhile you hunger for, yearn for, beg for aliens who look, well, *alien*. You want tentacles and one eye (or none!), and lots of dripping mucous, like in *The War of the Worlds*. At the very least you want something that you don't see kids dressing up as on Halloween.

So when you get a report of silent aliens that look like tin cans, it gets exciting again.

It began as so many cases have: in the road. James Townsend was a 19-year-old announcer for radio station KEYL in Long Prairie. The evening of Oct. 23, 1965, he was rounding a curve on Minnesota Highway 27, traveling from Little Falls. Townsend recalled to Air Force UFO consultant J. Allen Hynek that he was about four miles from Long Prairie when, "My car engine stalled, the lights and radio went out." He had just checked his watch—7:15 p.m.

There in front of him was a pillar of silver resting on three fins, an upright rocket, 30 or 40 feet high, 10 feet around. The car continued to coast until Townsend finally braked.

"I stopped about 20 feet in front of it," Townsend recalled. It was fantastic, incredible. But who would believe it?

"My first thought was to knock it over with the car so I could have some evidence," he said. The disabled rocket could then be seen by the authorities. He tried starting the car. It wouldn't start. Townsend then thought to tip the rocket—"try to rock the center of gravity and topple it over so that I would have the evidence right there in black and white."

He put his 1956-model car into "park" and got out.

"When I got to the front of my car, three creatures that looked like individual tin cans on tripods, and were 6 inches tall, came from behind the rocket. They didn't have any eyes that I could see, but I knew they were looking at me. I stopped. I didn't have any desire to get closer.

"They were brown or black, cylindrical in shape, had very thin 'arms' and walked on two 'fins.'" The objects moved with a side-to-side waddle. When they stopped, a third "fin" came down from the objects' rears.

"I know that I was looking at them and I was quite fascinated with what I saw. You might ask why, since I was willing to go up to them before, I did not go up to them now. I used what I hope was common sense. I felt that if they could stop my car, they could surely do something worse to me, and I wanted to live and tell the story so that the people of the United States would know that there were things of this nature.

"There was no sound—just dead silence. It seemed like ages, as we looked at each other.

"I can safely say that we 'looked' at each other for about three minutes.

"Then they went up into the rocket, which had a bright colorless light glowing out of the bottom. There was a loud hum."

The rocket, according to Townsend, began to rise, looking "just like a flashlight that is turned on and then lifted up from the table with the light at the bottom.

"When the light on the bottom went out after it was in the air, my car radio and light came on—and my engine started without having to touch the starter." The rocket had vanished.

"I looked at the area that it had been sitting on over and could see no evidence that it had been on the ground."

Townsend said his heart was pounding and his legs were like rubber as he drove into Long Prairie at 90 miles per hour. "I was sure of two things," he said. "The rocket was a spaceship of some kind, and the three objects that came out of it were creatures like nothing else in the animal world I have ever seen. They were definitely not people as I know them."

Raccoon hunters were out that night. Some reported a strong light passing overhead, lighting the ground around them. Four had even seen the object take off. The object also circled a farm several times, drawing the attention of its residents. And the sheriff of neighboring Anoka County reported having also seen the UFO.

Townsend drove to the Todd County Sheriff's Office and told them what he had seen. He later reported the encounter to the Air Force, as well. "I know that this is quite a wild story but if you do not believe me, well [expletive deleted from Air Force files] that's your tough luck."

The Air Force closed the case without formally looking into it—they regularly threw out reports dealing with aliens, judging them impossible on their face. But Hynek, the Air Force's special advisor, personally investigated. He talked with Todd County's Sheriff Bain, who vouched for Townsend's sobriety, Christianity and truthfulness. The sheriff and Long Prairie Police Officer Lavern Lubitz checked the spot the next day and found what appeared to be three parallel streaks of oil and water at the site. These were about four inches apart and a yard long.

"I don't know what they were," Sheriff Bain told reporters. "But I've looked at a lot of roads and never saw anything like them before."

The Aerial Phenomena Research Organization, a civilian investigative group, questioned Townsend's teachers and friends; all agreed

I BRAKE FOR ALIENS

J. Allen Hynek, Northwestern University astronomer and special advisor for the U.S. Air Force's UFO investigative unit, Project Blue Book, later commented in his book, *The Hynek UFO Report*, "It would almost appear that one's chances of seeing a UFO are greater if one is driving a car than if one is out in the open. In case after case, reports contain the phrase, 'after rounding a bend in the road.' While these objects are not always standing in the road, they do seem to do so often enough. When there is open countryside on either side of the road, one can't help but wonder why."

he was truthful. Hynek was disinclined to believe the story was a hoax.

I know of no other sighting where similar creatures were reported. I've tried, and failed, to find Townsend today. His is undoubtedly the best known close encounter of the third kind to come from Minnesota.

Was it real? I don't know. But I have heard rumors—just rumors—that the entire section of highway where the strange marks were left was quickly removed—by whom no one knows—soon after Townsend's sighting.

BIGFOOT

I n 1911 in northern Minnesota, two hunters found a trail of "strange" footprints and followed them to a "human giant" with long arms and short, dark hair on its body.

Bigfoot in Minnesota? Ha! Just a grandparent's tall tale designed to scare children. Such a thing might be reported in 1911 but not today. Right?

Well, how about this:

In early 1979 near Rochester, Larry Hawkins saw a Bigfoot crouching near a road. He stopped and the creature ran away, abandoning a dead rabbit upon which it had apparently been feeding. On Dec. 14, 1979, again near Rochester, a woman saw a 7-foot upright, hairy creature in the lights of her car. It covered its eyes with its arms.

Bigfoot is usually associated with the Pacific Coast, and a Minnesota Bigfoot would seem to be out of place. But the fabled creature has been seen many times in the Great Lakes region; in fact, immigrants to America first encountered the creature in the Midwest, not the West. In Michigan City, Ind., in the summer of 1839, a "wild child" reportedly haunted that city's Fish Lake, "setting up the most frightful and hideous yells," according to an early press account. Today we would call it a child Bigfoot.

Legends from Minnesota's Ojibwe (or Chippewa) Indians take the story back even further. They knew a creature that today we also would call Bigfoot. They called it Windigo.

The Rev. Peter Jones was a missionary traveling in 1831 through what later became Minnesota, and he knew firsthand of the Windigo. An Ojibwe himself, he had been taken from his tribe and taught by missionaries. But he never forgot his early childhood, when he had "often listened with wonder and deep attention to the stories related of the waindegoos (sic), or giants. They are represented as beings tall as pine trees .... In their travels they pull down and turn aside immense forests, as a man would the high grass as he passes through.

"They are said to live on human flesh, and whenever they meet an Indian are sure to have a good meal; being also invulnerable to the shot of an arrow or bullet, they are the constant dread of the Indians. Persons who have been known to eat human flesh from starvation are also called waindegoos, after the giants." (See opposite page.)

Indeed, "the Windigo are powerful giants," wrote Charles Brown, director of the State Historical Society of Wisconsin, who collected Ojibwe Windigo stories in 1927. It was part animal, a wild "man" who left footprints twice the normal size. The legends reported that the Windigo killed Indians for food, cut them up and boiled them in their kettles. "The belief in them still persists," Brown wrote.

Who were the Windigo? The Delaware Indians called creatures like them "Alligewi," after the Allegheny River. According to Delaware legends, the Alligewi once tried to migrate to the east, into the traditional Delaware territories. The Delaware went to war with the Alligewi. The Delaware supposedly fought the Alligewi down the Ohio River, then up the Mississippi, and then to Minnesota. The story is next picked up by the Minnesota Sioux, who have a legend about a race of giants that appeared there—and were killed.

Possibly, the Windigo legends refer to an earlier form of man— cave man. Neanderthal lived about 75,000 years ago and then inexplicably vanished. Could Native Americans have recalled the Neanderthal? After all, the Ojibwe and Dakota tribal memories extended far enough back to embrace the woolly mammoth. Elephant-like figures pepper the tribes' art, incredible as that may seem. And earlier forms of man are known to have lived alongside man-like cousins. In France,

BIGFOOT CAPITAL OF THE WORLD

Minnesota is home to the Bigfoot Capital of the World, the town of Crookston. If you visit, you can lunch on Bigfoot burgers, Bigfoot cookies, and even view a life-sized statue of the creature outside RBJ's Restaurant.

You can buy a Bigfoot doll for $20, Bigfoot jam for $4.75, and Bigfoot chocolates for $10. But you will apparently have little chance of seeing Bigfoot.

The Crookston Development Authority in 1995 took a report of unusual tracks near the Red Lake River and spun it into a publicity campaign for the town. Does this mean there are lots of sightings there?

"No, no," said Kim Samuelson, proprietor of RBJ's Restaurant and the Development Authority's Bigfoot expert. "We really don't have any information."

A disappointment—but I will say this much: the dolls look pretty cool.

archaeologists have for decades been puzzled by the fact that Neanderthal and Modern Man lived side by side. Could the Indian legends tell of a race of distant relatives to man who—at least at one time—really existed?

It would help, of course, if we had some hard evidence. This is the constant cry of skeptics, and rightfully so. It is one of my beliefs that we have abundant evidence of unexplained phenomena, it's just that the data is difficult to retrieve, organize and analyze.

Early excavations, long ignored, may offer the proof we need. On Aug. 12, 1896, The St. Paul *Globe* reported that "a huge man" was dug up on the Beckley farm on Lake Koronis. In Warren in 1882, 10 "gigantic bodies"; at Chatfield, seven 8-foot skeletons with skulls showing receding foreheads, the mouths full of double rows of teeth.

Were these reports merely newspaper hoaxes? Not according to the Minnesota Historical Society, which in 1911 published *The Aborigines of Minnesota*, an exceptionally weighty and overlooked volume.*

We learn of many excavations from *Aborigines of Minnesota*. In La Crescent, on the Mississippi, 52 mounds were excavated. "When opened they have been found to contain human remains of men of large stature, and it is said that in grading for the railroad a copper skillet and other trinkets were found at 18 feet below the surface." So reads the geological report on Houston County, part of a survey conducted in 1884.

At Dresbach, also on the Mississippi, around 1885, Indian mounds yielded 8-foot skeletons; similar skeletons had earlier been unearthed nearby. "Large human bones" were also excavated from the Lanesboro group of mounds in Fillmore County. There were 600 sets of skeletons, all of full-grown men—no women or children. George E. Powell, writing in 1907, said that 27 years earlier he had heard oral histories representing a battle to have occurred 200 years before then. The dead were supposedly strangers slain by Ojibwe; the story had come from a 100-year-old Ojibwe.

At Moose Island Lakes, an 1861 survey noted the recovery of 7-foot skeletons from mounds. At Pine City, a "gigantic" skeleton was exhumed. At Rainy River in 1896, a 9-foot skeleton was found.

These finds are extremely problematic. At least 40 million years ago there were indeed primates in North America, but only in Central

---

* To illustrate how embarrassingly obscure these early findings have become: I found *Aborigines of Minnesota* still in its original 1911 binding at the State Historical Society of Wisconsin. I was struck by the absence of a "return by" slip in the book. The library staff obligingly confirmed my suspicion: I am only the second person to have checked out the book in 86 years.

and South America have they survived until today. There they evolved in a manner very similar to their Old World relatives, small monkeys, and are unlikely to have given rise to a native population of Windigo, or—as it is called by Pacific Coast Indians—Sasquatch. Anthropologist Myra Shackley has pointed out, quite rightly, that since "there were no North American primates to evolve into Sasquatch, it would have evolved somewhere else and migrated to North America."

Of course, the fossil record does present numerous candidates for what possibly evolved into the Windigo. The Neanderthal is easily ruled out; even given evolution, its size is far too small to account for modern American sightings. (However, several scholars have very effectively argued the Neanderthal's survival in Asia, accounting for stories of the Abominable Snowman and similar creatures there.)

There is, nevertheless, an older form of man, *Gigantopithecus*, which evolved in Asia at least 9 million years ago, and which survived until at least 1 million years ago. It is possible that *Gigantopithecus* could have crossed a land bridge between Siberia and North America. That would have been a trip of merely 52 miles.

If it did, Shackley suggested such a migration occurred before the beginning of the Ice Age 1.8 million years ago. The reason for this is that the nearest probable relative to the Windigo, the Yeti or Abominable Snowman, is reportedly quite different. While the two may have shared common stock, *Gigantopithecus* needed a great deal more time on the American continent for evolution to change it to Sasquatch, distinct from its cousin, the Yeti. Of course, both the Yeti and Windigo could have evolved considerably *"in situ* since that time," Shackley pointed out, "but it does make sound geographical and zoological sense to suggest that their ultimate origins probably lie in the same population and general area."

By comparison, *Homo sapiens*—Modern Man—probably migrated during two relatively recent periods: one occurring 36,000 to 32,000 years ago, and another 28,000 to 13,000 years ago.

Wherever these creatures come from, Minnesotans have seen them. On Nov. 12, 1968, north of Floodwood, Uno Keikkile or Heikkile (accounts differ) was hunting 10 miles north of town. He sat down on a stump, and a 4^1/$_2$-foot Bigfoot dropped down from a tree. It was about 125 feet away. It walked off into the woods "on its back feet."

In early July 1972, near Tower, a 13-year-old girl, Debby Trucano, and a friend, saw a white 4^1/$_2$-foot Bigfoot in some woods. It was later seen by four others.

On Jan. 26, 1973, at Island Lake near Duluth, Bob McGregor, age 11, saw a white, furry Bigfoot walk across a yard and through an unfinished house. The creature was 8½-feet tall. In November 1978, Richard Johnson saw a similar creature in a swamp.

One night in July 1977 or '78, Chris Machmer was roughing it in the family cabin 12 miles east of Cotton, near Long Lake, when he thought he saw a Bigfoot look through the door. "This happened when I was very young, and it sounds incredible, but it happened," he said.

One thing is certain: the Windigo is just as mysterious today, in our scientific age, as ever.

Ever since his experience, Chris Machmer said, "there's the feeling I get when I'm in the woods. Kind of like I'm not really alone. Which is not to say that I feel that there is a (Windigo) in the woods wherever I go, it's just the knowledge that there is something else 'there,' in general ...."

HUMAN WINDIGO

We have to be careful in examining stories of the Windigo. The Ojibwe actually had two classes of Windigo. One was the beast, and the other was a human cannibal. The latter phenomenon is as interesting to me as the former, and since stories of both are sometimes difficult to separate, I think it will be useful to briefly examine the all-too-human Windigo as well as the animal one.

Both kinds of Windigo legends were studied by German writer Johann Georg Kohl, who traveled the Minnesota territory in 1855. He noted that the term "Windigo" was "much more frequently used with reference to the giant race of [human] cannibals known by the name, than to the [animal] monsters now having their being among us." But the monsters among us were common enough, and Kohl recorded many stories of mad and starving Ojibwe who had killed their own for food. This monstrous behavior bestowed monstrous status. The guilty individual was thereafter known as a Windigo himself or herself.

"Anyone that has once broken through the bounds (of cannibalism) does so easily again, or, at least, the supposition is rife that he can do so," Kohl wrote. "Hence he becomes an object of apprehension, and must live retired from the rest of his fellow men. He does not enjoy their fraternal assistance, and thus his hostile position towards society soon drives him back into the same difficulty and temptation. In this manner, or nearly so, a class of Windigos is called into existence."

One of Kohl's stories was about an Ojibwe man who had wandered the forests on the northern bank of a lake. "He was known perfectly well, and his name was even mentioned to me. I learnt that during a hard winter he had killed and eaten his squaw; after that he had attacked, killed, and also devoured a girl. This man always went about hunting by himself, and whenever his canoe was seen, the sight produced terror and alarm, and all the world fled from him. He was equally a burden to himself as to the others, and, in consequence of all the agony he endured, he had fallen into a state of brooding melancholy and a fearful affliction of the brain."

Indeed, wrote Kohl, the man's sufferings were so great that "his brain was quite softened, and the sutures of his temple had begun to give way." Ouch! Even as the story was told to Kohl, the Ojibwe were hunting the offender so that "he would before long receive a vengeful bullet from society."

It is no surprise, then, that in some stories, Windigos had families, with brothers, sisters and spouses. A Windigo and an Indian could even marry, though as a rule the couple would not be welcome in the village. This was obviously not the Bigfoot-type of Windigo.

Interestingly, Kohl believed there was even a sort of Windigo-inspired mental illness. "The people's fancy is so busy with them, as well as with the isolated cases of real cannibalism, that they begin to dream of them, and these dreams, here and there, degenerate to such a point that a man is gained over to the idea that he is fated to become a Windigo.

"Such dreams vary greatly. At times a man will merely dream that he must kill so many persons during his life; another dream adds that he must also devour them; and as these strange beings believe in their dreams as they do in the stars, they act in accordance with their gloomy suggestions.

"The Windigo mania rarely breaks out spontaneously; it must have its predecessors and degrees. If a man lives much apart and out of the world, if he appears to be melancholy and is tortured by evil dreams, then people begin to fear he may be becoming a Windigo, and he is himself attacked by the fatalistic apprehension, and is driven towards a gloomy fate. At times, when a man is quarreling with his wife, he will say, 'Squaw, take care. Thou wilt drive me so far that I shall turn Windigo.'"

For example, Kohl reports, in the early 1850s an Ojibwe man dreamed that he had to kill seven men in his life. He would not be able to stop until he had reached seven. The man didn't want to do it, resisted doing it—couldn't comprehend doing it. But the dreams continued, "and so soon as opportunity offered, he killed a fellow-being."

He killed twice more. His crimes were still secret, but some suspected—his closest friends, for example, with whom he had shared the stories of his mad dreams. "And so, as he was sitting one day with his back to a tree, brooding and solitary, an axe cleft the wicked dreamer's head asunder. A few of his victim's friends had joined together to put him out of the way. They did so, and the whole community applauded them for freeing them from such a monster."

Incredibly, while visiting an Ojibwe village Kohl was told of another visitor, an Ojibwe man named Missabikongs, who had recently been turned away for fear of what he might be becoming.

"Do you believe the man is a Windigo?" asked Kohl.

"No; not yet—perhaps not yet!" was his host's reply.

The human Windigos were believed to be supernatural— they had an understanding with evil spirits, who help them." Although the human Windigos might escape detection for a time, they were at least easy to kill. "A real [non-human] Windigo is very difficult to kill ... in order to destroy him thoroughly, he must be torn to pieces. Otherwise, he may easily come to life again." The similarity here to stories of European vampirism is striking. Another parallel is the Windigo's—and vampire's—hope for peace through salvation. One human Windigo Kohl had heard of "was converted to Christianity, confessed his sins, and died as a Christian."

Ahem.

THE GIANT BUNNIES
OF LAKE WOBEGON

I have tried your patience with Bigfoot. You have wondered about my gullibility when it comes to flying saucers. I have added cave man bones to Indian legends and come up with Bigfoot. But I have yet to offer you the strangest, the most odd, the most amazing ... giant bunnies!

Actually, Minnesota's jumping creatures were only once described as giant bunnies. The rest of the time they were described as kangaroos. They have been seen in Coon Rapids, and near Anoka, hometown of humorist Garrison Keillor and the inspiration for his Lake Wobegon.

In 1957, Barbara Battmer's two sons, ages 7 and 9, were playing in a forested area near Coon Rapids, off Highway 10, when they saw two kangaroos hopping together. They claimed ever since that the kangaroos were 5 feet tall, and that they crossed a small clearing about 50 feet away. They were light tan and medium brown.

Linda Brodie, another Coon Rapids resident, told Loren Coleman, one of America's foremost "cryptozoologists," that she had also seen a kangaroo in 1958.* Mrs. Gary Haider told him that in the same year, her two brothers came home with reports of a "big rabbit" they had seen hopping around.

And Hazel and Willard Hayes saw two oversized "bunnies" on the evening of April 24, 1967, in an open area about a mile west of Highway 47, near the Anoka County Fairgrounds.

If Minnesota does have kangaroos, one would reasonably assume that they do not respect state boundaries. A skeptic would argue that reports of such misplaced animals could be taken somewhat more seriously if there were similar reports from—oh, say, Wisconsin.

Well, Wisconsin has kangaroo reports, nine of them, to be exact. Just across the Minnesota border, in Eau Claire County, a woman saw a kangaroo on Highway 12, between Augusta and Fall Creek, on May 21, 1978. Mark Hall, a Minnesota investigator of sightings of strange and apparently misplaced animals, has examined plaster casts of tracks left by a Wisconsin kangaroo. The casts were of tracks around 6 inches long and 3 inches wide. "Generally the tracks have a two-pronged fork appearance with two knobs at the rear of the 'fork handle,'" Hall said.

One Wisconsin kangaroo was even photographed near Waukesha in 1978. (The photo and full accounts of the sightings are included in my book of Wisconsin's unexplained phenomena, *The W-Files.*) Coleman describes the Polaroid photo as showing "a tan animal with lighter brown front limbs, hints of a lighter brown hind limb, dark brown or black patches around the eyes, inside the two upright ears, and possibly surrounding the nose and upper mouth area." He compares it favorably to Bennett's wallaby, or brush kangaroo, native to Tasmania, where it ranges from lower valleys to snowy summits.

Kangaroos, or something like them, have appeared in many other parts of the central United States, and if their sense of geography is strange, so is their behavior. In January 1934, an incredibly fast kangaroo attacked dogs, geese and ducks in rural Tennessee. The Chattanooga *Daily Times* concluded, "There is absolutely no doubt about these facts. A kangaroo-like beast visited the community and killed

---

* Coleman collected these Minnesota reports and interviewed the witnesses. He has generously shared his information with me. I have tried, and not surprisingly have failed, to find these Minnesotans for updates 30 years after the last sighting.

dogs ... and that's all there is to it."

This, as well as some of the wilder Wisconsin reports of two-legged hopping creatures, makes me doubt that these stories report true kangaroos. I think they are historical reports of what has since become known as the Chupacabras. Some "Chupas" reports make it out to be a 7- or 8-foot Bigfoot, but most often it sounds a lot like a kangaroo—a mean kangaroo, but a kangaroo. The Chupacabras, or "goat-sucker," made its mysterious debut in Puerto Rico in 1995. Since then it has been blamed for leaving a trail littered with dead livestock in Florida, Massachusetts, New York, New Jersey, Texas and California. The livestock attacks are distinct from classic cattle mutilations, however. Chupas attacks livestock, puncturing the necks, suggesting that it may feed on the victim's blood. The marks are made by the upper teeth. There are no corresponding marks showing similar teeth on the lower jaw.

Part of the puzzle is that there supposedly is no established tradition of the Chupacabras. Things like lake monsters, Bigfoot, vampires and so on have a long history. If we didn't call them by the names we have today, at least there is a suggested counterpart in folklore. Not so with the Chupacabras. It literally came out of nowhere, leading some to theorize that it is an escaped genetic experiment or an alien creature sent to demonize us, or both.

Its description, especially in early reports, varies. It is supposed to have fur, or it is supposed to have feathers, or it has a lizard's scales, or a toad's bumps. It is almost always upright, though, and it has a muzzle and small arms and hands. And it is shaped like a kangaroo, and its tracks show three toes, as did the plaster casts of Wisconsin's kangaroo. One report has it able to jump a 6-foot fence.

The Chupacabras has been seen by various people, including Puerto Rican officials. In Sweetwater, Fla., where it was seen in March 1996, it was described as "a dog-like figure standing up, with two short hands in the air." In May 1996, it was seen in Arizona, where it apparently "mumbled and gestured." In June 1996, it was spotted in the Sonora Desert of Mexico, where witnesses described it as "like a turkey or kangaroo."

In fact, in the Campo Rico district of Puerto Rico, it is not called Chupacabras at all, but is referred to as "el canguro." Guess what that translates as?

UFOS BEFORE
THERE WERE UFOS

On the night of April 11, about a thousand residents of Minneapolis looked up and saw a UFO.

The next day's paper reported, "Everyone who saw the aerial visitor last night hastened to the telephone to tell the newspapers about it. Judging by the number of telephone calls there is no use printing anything because the people have seen and know all that there is to know."

It didn't happen last year, or even in this century. It happened in 1897. The sightings are impossible to explain in terms of the period's level of technology.

At the close of the 19th century, thousands of people saw strange things in the sky, attributing them sometimes to aliens but more often to secretive inventors, including experimenters traveling with the Ringling Bros. circus. The sightings began in late April 1896 in California and spread east. "In major cities like Sacramento, Omaha and Chicago, thousands rushed into the streets or clambered to rooftops to view the vessel as it passed," wrote Daniel Cohen in his history of the phenomenon, *The Great Airship Mystery*.

People have seen strange things in the sky since Biblical times, coming up with explanations that fit their cultures, technologies and theologies. It wasn't until 1947 that extraterrestrials were given the cultural nod. Just 50 years before that, hovering cigar-shaped objects were usually believed to be man-made inventions, something like dirigibles. But while dirigible technology was fairly advanced in 1896—an experimental craft flew successfully in France in 1882—a practical, maneuverable airship was not yet on the scene. Historically, the sightings are impossible to explain in terms of the first navigable aircraft, dirigibles.

Since 1854, the Rev. William Markoe had been trying to invent just such an airship in St. Paul. His "Aeroport," designed with Rufus Porter of Washington, D.C., never got off the ground—so far as we know, though its plans were so complete as to include a budget that outlined both weight and cost:

Cloth for float—400 yards	200 lbs	$200
1,200 feet of rods	200 lbs	10
Saloon, 25 feet long	200 lbs	50
Connecting wires and rudder	100 lbs	50
Propelling wheels	100 lbs	30
Labor in making the float		50
Cost of inflation		110
Total weight and cost:	800 lbs	$500

This particular design was to be 120 feet long, 20 feet in diameter, and 1,300 lbs. of "buoyant power," with a hand crank for a motor. It was never built. Markoe did, however, build a conventional balloon and in 1857 became the first Minnesotan to fly.

Just 14 years later, circuses featured balloon ascensions as regular attractions. From 1871 through about 1894, circus balloons were not uncommon, but they stayed close to the fairgrounds. Circuses could not account for the swift comings and goings of the mystery airship. It wasn't until 1905 that Pawnee Bill's Wild West Show featured a slow, tiny, self-propelled airship. It could not compare to the mystery airship of more than a decade earlier.

One of the first mystery airship sightings anywhere occurred on the night of Nov. 22, 1896, in Sacramento. Walter Mallory, a deputy sheriff, described it as "a strong white light" with a dark body immediately over it. At 1 p.m. the airship was sighted in Tacoma, Wash. A mere half hour later it was seen in San Jose, Calif., 750 miles away. The next evening it was in Los Angeles. Sightings continued all over the state.

William Randolph Hearst's *San Francisco Examiner* initially ignored the excitement, but at last announced on Nov. 28, "The biggest problem of the age has been solved. Man has won his hardest battle with nature. A successful airship has been built."

On Feb. 2, 1897, the airship appeared in Hastings, Neb. Three days later it was sighted 40 miles south in Invale, Neb. On March 27 it was in Topeka, Kan., where it was seen by several hundred people, including the state's governor.

On April 4 it was sighted in Wisconsin, but then it backtracked and on the 10th it appeared in Keokuk, Iowa. Sightings continued in Texas, Arkansas, Missouri, Wisconsin and Illinois. The mystery airship had a rugged schedule, suggesting either incredible speed or the presence of a whole fleet.

Newspapers in Chicago tracked the airship and predicted its speed. They announced that it would arrive around April 9, and it did. It stayed in the area three days, long enough to be photographed. Sadly, the photo has been lost, though hand-drawn copies survive.

It arrived in Minneapolis on the night of April 10, but the best descriptions come from the next night. Most observers said they saw a bright light that changed from red to green to white and back again. One businessman, R.G. Adams, said he had used field glasses on the object and had observed the lights attached to the cigar-shaped craft. He told the *Pioneer Press* that he had seen it flying low at around 8 p.m. in the direction of Minnetonka. His mother and father saw it, too. The newspaper found him at the corner of Lake Street and Nicollet Avenue, "with an excited crowd of men and boys, a few of whom had seen the flying machine." The witnesses included R.K. Melville and L.B. Davis. Yet another man, H. Webb Chamberlain, called the paper from near the same intersection and gave a running commentary of his observations. All agreed on the description afterward given by Adams.

"Through the glass I saw an object that appeared to be 18 or 20 feet long," Adams said. "It was shaped like a cigar and in the middle and on top of it was a square light .... He was going at a high rate of speed when I saw him. He would dip and shoot down for, say a half mile with a green light, and then mount with the speed of a rocket showing a white light. As he floated he changed his light to red or green."

The phenomenon of colors changing with the motion of UFOs has since become a repeatedly observed characteristic.

"The light looked as big as a plate through the glass, but to the naked eyes appeared about the size of an orange," Adams said. "I could distinctly see the vague outlines of the craft."

Whatever it was, it was seen from several points in the Twin Cities, and it departed around 8:50 p.m. for Lake Minnetonka. There it was seen by a druggist, a Mr. Newell of Excelsior, who spoke to the *Pioneer Press* by telephone as he viewed the object.

"It seems to be coming toward Excelsior from the direction of Hotel St. Louis," he said. "We can see a green and a white light. Sometimes it takes a shoot down and we see the green light plainly. Then it rises slowly up. It dodges around and sometimes seems to go almost in a circle."

In Excelsior another witness got a view of the craft's outline. "Mrs. Dr. Small looked at it through a field glass, and through the hazy atmosphere was able to discern a dark body which moved with the light. It would move very erratically, shooting downward and to one side, and then rising with a succession of jerky motions."

The same night, the airship—or one like it—visited Albert Lea. Ex-mayor Gillrup said he saw it at 10:30 p.m., and the light moved up and down and sideways and then disappeared to the northwest. It was seen by "a large number," according to a special dispatch to the *Pioneer Press*. "The suggestion that it is from the planet Mars is not generally believed, but those seeing the strange light declare it is no illusion."

On the 12th the airship visited Duluth, where residents had gathered on top of a building block with field glasses. Around 9:30 p.m. they observed several rapidly moving lights in the west. The *Pioneer Press* said, "there is much diversity of opinion as to the number (of lights), but one of the observers says that with one eye closed he could see at least three distinct airships in outline, spread out like a flock of geese. The night was too thick for good observation, but if there is a fleet of airships it may be that all the places that have reported seeing the same airship may have seen different ones."

Indeed, the airship swept the state, first visiting Taylors Falls on Feb. 6, then Waseca on April 9. On the 10th it was first seen at Anoka, Lake Crystal and Minneapolis—once a community had been visited by

THREE RINGS OF UFOS

There is one plausible earthbound explanation for the airship: it belonged to the Ringling Bros. circus.

The explanation, denied by the circus, came when a Madison, Wis., newspaper pointed out that the airship's appearance in Chicago occurred "almost simultaneously with the advent to that city of the Ringlings." One of the brothers was even observed transporting "large and mysterious bundles" from the circus grounds.

A reporter sent from Madison to the circus's base of operations, in Baraboo, Wis., found that residents there were "of the opinion that the airship was a succession of balloons or something of the kind, which were aimed to prey upon the curiosity of an incredulous public to the end that shining half dollars would pour into the big wagons where tickets for the big show are sold."

On April 15 the Chicago *Times-Herald* stated that the airship was definitely the product of the Ringlings' Baraboo workshops, where it was still being tested and perfected. The article said that the airship was based on a model created by a New York inventor, built by a man named Carr and further developed by the Ringlings.

The Ringling Bros. denied it, and so does a leading circus

historian today.

"I've never heard of any dirigible experiments with the Ringling show," said Fred Dahlinger, Jr., director of the circus library and research center at Baraboo's Circus World Museum, housed in the very workshops where the airship was allegedly created. "I really would find it hard to believe that any show at that time would do anything with dirigibles," he told me.

the airship, later sightings were almost certain. On the 11th it was first seen in Excelsior, Minnetonka, Montgomery, Preston and Winona. The airship had a much lighter schedule on the 12th. Besides Duluth, as mentioned above, it only traveled to the Minnesota communities of Jonesville and Virginia. We'll skip the 13th for now; on the 14th it visited Windom; the 15th, Essig and Sleepy Eye; the 18th, Elbow Lake; the 19th, New Ulm; and the 21st, Fergus Falls.

One of the strangest things about the airship, obviously, was that it alternated busy nights with slow nights. You would expect phenomena merely imagined by a hysterical mob to have a relatively constant number, without odd-day highs and even-day lows.

The night of the 13th, which we momentarily skipped, was exceptionally busy, with airship visits to Bigelow, Breckenridge, Hastings, Hector, Lake Lillian, Madison Lake, Mankato, Norwood and Young America. It also visited Hudson and Royalton, which we'll now look at in detail.

The *Pioneer Press* reported that on the 13th the airship had also been seen in Stillwater. There the observers were telegraph operators "along the Omaha line in the vicinity of this city .... At Stillwater Junction only lights were seen, but at Northern Wisconsin Junction the operators claim they saw the outline of the ship, which was cigar-shaped."

At Royalton the same night, 50 people watched the airship for 20 minutes beginning around 9 p.m. In Winona, Harry Friday and several others described the airship as a "soapy bubble."

Also on the 13th, "two truthful citizens," Frederick Chamberlain, of Hudson, Wis., and O.I. Jones, of New Sweden, encountered the airship on the ground on "the road to Hudson."

"Soon after 11 o'clock we were about a mile this side of Lake Kimo when, looking off one side of the road and into an opening into the woods, we saw a man walking about with a lantern," Chamberlain said the next day. "He walked around and around, as if he was looking for something. There was no house near. The moon, you recollect, was shining brightly last night. We could see quite distinctly except for the shadows from the trees. So we thought something had gone wrong to keep a man busy with a lantern in so lonely a spot.

"Jones said, 'Let's drive in there.'

"'All right,' says I, and we turned our team—it was a two-horse buggy we had—off towards the clearing about two blocks distant. We hadn't gone five rods before the lantern suddenly disappeared.

We heard a crackling of twigs and brush from the clearing. Then a rushing noise—irregular, more like wind blowing around the eaves of a house than escaping steam. A second later and we distinguished a long, high object of a gray white color. The thing struck me as resembling most the top of a 'prairie schooner' or immigrant wagon covered with canvas. At the same instant we saw two rows of lights—four lights in two pairs—one pair including a red and green light. The thing rose quickly at a sharp angle, so as to just clear the tree tops.

"As it passed over the trees to the south we saw several more white lights. But we could make out no machinery or wings or wheels or rudders, or human figures, or even the exact outline of the affair. Fact was, it went up all in a jiffy, and we were too surprised to get a good view.

"Almost immediately after we saw the object it vanished behind the trees. The timber was right alongside us, and cut off our view.

"Jones said then, 'Why, man, that must be the airship!' I hadn't even thought of such a possibility, although, of course, I've heard of the mystery. Anyway, we drove over to the clearing. It was rather wet ground and in the mud were 14 marks ...."

Each of the marks was 2 feet long and 6 inches wide, arranged in two curving rows of seven, forming an oblong.

"But there was nothing else around that we could see in the bad light, though we looked for something accidentally left behind."

Adam Thielen, a farmer who lived near Elmo, also heard the buzzing sound around the same time and saw "a dark object high in the sky and bearing red and green lights."

To me, this airship sighting is the best I have ever found, nationwide. There was more than one witness. They not only saw the airship, but heard it, too. The witnesses could easily have added details—others often "saw" wings, propellers and even gears—and yet they did not. In fact, they refused even to describe the airship's sound in terms of the only mechanical force that could have explained it at the time—steam. They did, however, include unimportant details, such as the number of horses they had. And Chamberlain's initial inability to connect what he saw with the airship stories is a reaction I've observed in witnesses many times: those who sight modern UFOs usually are just puzzled at the time, perhaps stunned with incredulity. Only in retrospect do they realize they have seen a UFO.

There were other disappointing reports from the period, as well, and at least one copycat hoaxer. A "small boy with a genius for mechanics" had sent up a balloon with just such lights, according to the *Minneapolis Journal*. Maybe that accounts for the sightings—and maybe not.

Finally, on April 19 the *Minneapolis Tribune* topped its St. Paul rival, the *Pioneer Press,* by proudly announcing that one of its own reporters had encountered not only the airship, but also its crew.

"I rushed out to them," wrote the unnamed journalist, who had stumbled upon the airship in some woods. "Seeing me, they came at me like wild beasts, but I drew my revolver and warned them to stand and deliver their secret. Thereupon one of them introduced himself as J.S. McMasters of Chicago and admitted that he was the inventor of the craft which had excited so much wonder."

McMasters explained that the airship operated on the principle of "negative gravity."

This episode was almost certainly a hoax designed to cast doubt on the truthfulness of previous reports, given the reporter's closing paragraph: "When I told my story, they said I was crazy and they had me locked up. I am writing this from jail, but I am as sane as any man and never wrote a fake any more than Sioux City and Omaha reporters."

At least, I hope this was a hoax. I'm a reporter of the unexplained myself, and I don't want to go to jail.

LAND OF 10,000
FLYING SAUCERS

Well, maybe not 10,000, but we're talking a heap of UFOs, anyway. What follows is a list of every Minnesota UFO report I could get my hands on.

A word about the terminology: the study of UFOs, casually referred to as "ufology," does have a rudimentary science to it, thanks in large part to the efforts of two leaders in the field, computer scientist Jacques Vale, formerly an advisor to NASA, and astronomer J. Allen Hynek, who for many years served as a special advisor to the U.S. Air Force's UFO investigative unit, Project Blue Book. He later went on to found his own private UFO research group. Both men created classification systems for the cursory discussion of what previously had been summarized only as flying saucers or flying discs. For our purposes, I am using Hynek's system.

"UFO," for unidentified flying object, is a euphemism and an acronym coined by the U.S. Air Force; it was applied by the military to objects only *before* they were studied; as in, "the UFO turned out to be a weather balloon." If, after study, the sighting still defied description, the Air Force dropped the UFO label and called it an "unknown."

Private ufologists, however, tend to reserve the term "UFO" for objects that survive scrutiny, as in "the bright, shining object was not Venus, but was a UFO." In the following listings of UFOs, I use the term only in the sense that the object was unidentified to the witness; it may be that many of the reports have more conventional explanations. Where the cases have survived Air Force scrutiny, I have noted that fact; the vast majority of these reports were not, however, reported to the Air Force in the first place. (And since 1969 the Air Force has refused to examine civilian reports. Rather strict regulations still require that reports of UFOs sighted by military personnel today be made within military channels. Failure to do so may result in incarceration.)

Hynek's two classification systems have gained currency in popular culture, without producing a lot of understanding. The first describes the object's appearance:

- *Nocturnal light*—By far the most common sort of sighting, this can look like a star or a planet, which is often what it turns out to be. It's not reserved for night, but can also occur in the morning and evening, in which case Venus is a very likely suspect.
- *Daylight disc*—This is our old friend the flying saucer, which in reality (well, the reality of UFOs, at least) comes in a bewildering variety of shapes and sizes; boomerang, triangle, cross, cigar—you name it, someone sometime has seen it. As Hynek points out, distant daylight discs may account for nocturnal lights, and it is also true that during the day some UFOs appear to be simply fast-moving points of light. Strangely, the most-often reported shapes of objects change over time, with fair consistency. It's almost as if new makes and models come out and are bought by style-conscious aliens; this, in fact, has been the conclusion of some Air Force personnel. These days triangular craft are reported with greater and greater frequency, replacing the classic domed platter.
- *Radar sighting*—UFOs on radar screens are not as rare as you might think, although these days they are quite a bit rarer than they once were, since civilian airport radars no longer "paint" all airborne objects and return the signals. Instead, they look for the radar transponders aboard aircraft. But even earlier in aviation history, a radar return did not provide certain knowledge of a UFO, as temperature inversions and other atmospheric pecu-

liarities could give a false return. Radar-visual sightings, on the other hand, with radar returns and eyewitness observation, are hard to argue with. Military radars, of course, still look for everything.

Hynek's second and better-known classification system ordered the proximity and behavior of the observed UFO in relation to the witness:

- *Close encounter of the first kind:* The big necessity here is proximity—just a couple of hundred feet. As opposed to the distant disc-shaped light, with this type of sighting we can see some details and perceive depth. Therefore, stars, aircraft, etc., are almost certainly ruled out.

- *Close encounter of the second kind*—This type of UFO is seen to interact with the viewer or environment. It follows our car, avoids intercepting aircraft, changes course in a logical manner. Landing marks may be made, grass may be charred, or debris may fall from the object—the so-called gossamer threads of "angel hair" that, theoretically, are made of ionized air sleeting off an electromagnetic field surrounding the object. The skeptics' constant call for hard evidence begins to be answered here; the Chicago-based Center for UFO Studies has logged more than 800 of these physical trace cases.

- *Close encounter of the third kind*—With this type, entities are observed, and we may now safely call the objects "craft," for they are certainly occupied, and probably even piloted by the occupants. Everything from Bigfoot to Nordic humans in ski suits have been seen in or around UFOs. Strangely, there are very few bizarre monsters. They mostly resemble humans— thus they are "humanoids." It may be that nature selects for human characteristics in all worlds where intelligence has risen. Or it may be that the "aliens" are actually humans coming back from the future. These days, no thoughtful student of UFOs jumps to conclusions. We are in the data-gathering stage and are obviously unable to test any hypothesis. Still, the most commonly reported alien in the United States is the "gray," a slim naked lad with no genitalia, no nose, a swollen head and wraparound eyes. (In Great Britain, the most commonly reported alien is the Nordic.)

After Hynek's death, another rank was added, *close encounters of the fourth kind*, encompassing the abduction phenomena.

UFOs are incredibly common in the upper Midwest. One U.S. Air Force summary shows that with the exception of a section of New Mexico, the north central part of the country has the largest number of unexplained sightings.

I apologize here for the sketchiness of some of the listings. I have given extended descriptions for unusually novel sightings. In some cases I have tried, unsuccessfully, to find more material on certain sightings, and have only the information given here. There are huge gaps in the microfilmed records of Minneapolis newspapers, for example, and countless mergers and publication names combined four times make the job even more difficult. I have not included reports that are bogus on their face, or reports that I believe have been reasonably explained.

For myself, the strongest evidence in favor of the reality of UFOs comes, simply, from the large number of reports. Can all of the following witnesses have been wrong? Could at least one of them have been right? It's for that reason I have chosen to emphasize the vast number of reports rather than just those I have been able to study in depth.

Here they are:

AITKIN, DEC. 5, 1960: Oliver Bakken observed a nocturnal light south of town.

ALBERT LEA, APRIL 8–10, 1897: The "mystery airship" was seen over several nights.

ALBERT LEA, EARLY JULY 1947: William Schultz saw one of Minnesota's first UFOs of the modern era over the Rock Island railroad station. "I knew it wasn't a plane," he said. "I could see its round shape."

ANOKA, APRIL 10–11, 13, 1897: The town that later would be fictionalized as Lake Wobegon was among those visited by the "mystery airship" over several evenings.

ANOKA, JAN. 6, 1976: A woman experienced a close encounter of the first kind.

AUSTIN, JUNE 4, 1963: Nocturnal light observed.

AUSTIN, JAN. 27, 1969: The Freeborn County Sheriff's Department investigated a UFO report.

AUSTIN, JAN. 1, 1976: UFO observed.

BAGLEY, APRIL 22, 1966: A witness experienced a close encounter of the third kind.

BEAVER LAKE, MARCH 22, 1978: Jeane Pluff experienced a close encounter of the first kind.

BIGELOW, APRIL 13, 1897: The "mystery airship" paid a visit.

BIWABIK, JULY 1978: A nocturnal light is observed.

BLAINE, AUG. 3, 1965: A nocturnal light is observed.

BLAINE, AUG. 24, 1975: A nocturnal light is observed.

BRECKENRIDGE, APRIL 13, 1897: The "mystery airship" was seen.

BROOKSTON, NOV. 20, 1954: A nocturnal light was observed—which seemed to crash into some woods; possibly a meteor.

BURNSVILLE, OCTOBER 1978: Ruth M. Dutton observed a nocturnal light.

BYRON, 4:45 a.m. MAY 30, 1995: A man observed a bright object in the sky that moved "strangely, fast." It approached a second "star" and both rose very quickly and disappeared. The man was described by the National UFO Reporting Center, a private group that took his report, as "alarmed."

CARVER COUNTY, OCT. 18, 1973: A nocturnal light was observed.

CEDAR, JAN. 6, 1976: Janet Stewart experienced a close encounter of the second kind on County Road 15.

CHISAGO CITY, SEPT. 11, 1974: Dale Olson observed a nocturnal light two miles south of town.

CHISHOLM, 9:55 a.m. SEPT. 25, 1965: Brett Diamon saw five orange lights in a row fly fast and make an abrupt turn during a one-minute sighting. This sighting was evaluated by the U.S. Air Force's Project Blue Book, which classified it as "unknown."

CLOQUET, JUNE 20, 1976: The witness had a close encounter of the second kind near Highway 35-W.

COMSTOCK, MAY 5, 1964: Alfred Ernst experienced a close encounter of the second kind.

COOK, MARCH 24, 1966: The witness experienced a close encounter of the second kind.

COON RAPIDS, APRIL 10, 1978: Bessie Wilson observed a nocturnal light on Highway 10.

COTTONWOOD, NOV. 29, 1956: Harold Thompson experienced a close encounter of the first kind.

COTTONWOOD, DEC. 25, 1960: As did the three wise men, Roger Birner got an unusual Christmas gift—the observation of a nocturnal light. He and his family were visiting relatives when, at about 11:45 p.m., he went outside for some air. He saw a light moving to the north. It came closer, and after about 30 seconds he could make out some detail: the object was very large and was shaped like a "half ball," with a dome on top. Light shone from the dome. At the base was an opening that seemed to reveal part of the interior, which looked like white string. The body of the craft was tan and had a silvery glow. The UFO descended by rocking gently from side to side—a classic action UFO researchers have nicknamed "falling leaf motion." It came down at an angle and stopped, hovering. Then it ejected a whitish object about the size of a pea held at arm's length. The smaller object floated to the west, until it appeared "about the size of a star." Then the first object went straight down and let out two more objects. These were red and the same size as the earlier small object. After clearing the presumed mother ship, the two red objects flew southeast, always maintaining the same distance apart. They appeared to flash green beams of light to each other. After several such exchanges, the two parted company and went in separate directions. The mother ship traveled toward one of the departing red objects, then stopped briefly and began heading in the opposite direction, bobbing up and down. Next it shot up twice as high as its previous apparent altitude, where it hovered. The red objects returned to the mother ship's interior. The small white object then also returned. Finally the "port" closed and the mother ship left in the direction from which it had come. The sighting had lasted from 10 to 15 minutes.

CRYSTAL, JAN. 16, 1978: Jon Spizale observed a nocturnal light on Maryland Avenue North.

CYRUS, NOV. 16, 1965: Tom Untiedt experienced a close encounter of the second kind on Highway 28.

DETROIT LAKES, NOV. 16, 1956: This community was one of many in Minnesota and South Dakota where an object like a ball of flame was observed. The 25-day UFO "flap" (series of sightings) began Nov. 8. See the Nov. 25, 1956, sighting at Reading.

DILWORTH, SEPT. 25, 1954: Many people observed a soaring blue-white ball of fire—possibly a meteor.

DULUTH, APRIL 12, 1897: The "mystery airship" paid a visit.

DULUTH, MARCH 13, 1959: UFO observed.

DULUTH, AUG. 4, 1965: A rare radar-visual sighting of a UFO was made.

DULUTH, AUG. 17, 1966: Dennis Tyo observed a nocturnal light near West Tischer Road.

DULUTH, AUG. 16, 1966: James Luhm experienced a close encounter of the second kind near Highway 8.

DULUTH, OCT. 7, 1973: A UFO was observed to hide behind a cloud —arguably, this was a close encounter of the second kind: acting on the environment.

EAGLE BEND, MAY 10, 1961: Richard Vogt experienced a close encounter of the second kind south of town.

EDEN PRAIRIE, NOV. 9, 1965: Leroy Hattery observed a nocturnal light near the airport.

EDEN PRAIRIE, APRIL 26, 1978: Sally Stoddart experienced a close encounter of the first kind near Baker Road.

ELBOW LAKE, APRIL 18, 1897: The "mystery airship" paid a visit.

ERSKINE, NOV. 16, 1965: Nocturnal light observed.

ESSIG, APRIL 15, 1897: The "mystery airship" was seen.

EXCELSIOR, APRIL 11, 1897: A Mr. Newell saw the "mystery airship."

EXCELSIOR, DEC. 1, 1971: A glowing object was seen moving against the southwest horizon shortly before midnight by 15 police officers in five towns, including Excelsior. "Too many of us saw it," said Excelsior policeman Mike Weber. "It had to be some-thing." The glowing sphere was about 1,000 feet up. Its color changed from red to green. It also hovered over Chanhassen. One police officer photographed it using a telephoto lens. Some said it was silent, others said they heard a humming sound.

FAIRFAX, OCT. 19, 1967: UFO observed.

FARIBAULT, OCTOBER 1977: Nocturnal light observed.

FARMINGTON, 7:50 p.m. OCT. 2, 1995: A man saw a very small, very bright light descending rapidly in the northeast. The light had an apparent diameter one-tenth that of the moon.

FARWELL, JANUARY 1967: Robert Blaine experienced a close encounter of the second kind two miles east of town on Highway 55.

FERGUS FALLS, APRIL 21, 1897: The "mystery airship" visited.

FERGUS FALLS, SEPT. 1, 1975: Nocturnal light observed.

FINLAND, JULY 1978: Nocturnal light observed.

FINLAND, SEPT. 5–6, 1966: Finland Air Force Base is 60 miles northeast of Duluth. From 9:30 p.m. on the fifth to 12:15 the next morning, reports of a "white-red-green" object "moving but not leaving its general location" were received at the base. Search radar did detect an object that "flitted around in range from 13 to 54 miles, but always stayed on the 270-degree azimuth." From a University of Colorado study, commissioned by the Air Force: "A pair of F-89s (interceptors) was scrambled from Duluth Air Force Base and searched the area at altitudes of 8,000 to 10,000 feet. The two aircraft 'merged with blip, apparently wrong altitude, no airborne sighting'; the radar operators insisted the target was at 8,000 to 10,000 feet, the same altitude at which the scrambled aircraft were flying. The pilots reported that they 'only observed what was interpreted to be a beacon reflection.'" The next evening, at 11, the investigating officer at Finland Air Force Base saw the same object in the same location. "This officer observed it and determined it to be a star which was near the horizon and would settle beneath the horizon after midnight," he wrote. "It did appear to 'sparkle' in red-green-white colors, but so do other stars which can be pointed out from this mountain top." Uh huh. The university researchers felt that the radar return was a false echo caused by an air inversion in the vicinity—a coincidence. The star's "strong red-green scintillation, apparent stretching of the image into a somewhat oval shape, and the red fringe on the bottom, may have been due to strong and irregular local refraction effects in the inversion layer (or layers)." The study also admitted, "there is no direct physical evidence for the existence" of such layers, "but no studies have been made to determine whether or not they might exist." I think this is pretty funny.

FLOODWOOD, MARCH 1967: Nocturnal light observed.

FOREST LAKE, DEC. 2, 1956: A Mr. Moffett observed a nocturnal light.

FOREST LAKE, OCT. 28, 1975: Nocturnal light observed.

FOREST LAKE, AUG. 19, 1995: A man waking with two strange cuts on his cheek called the sheriff's office to report a recurring dream of alien abduction.

FORT RIPLEY, NOV. 16, 1965: Russell Nelson observed a nocturnal light.

GARVIN, NOV. 26, 1966: John Nelson experienced a close encounter of the first kind near Lake Sarah.

GLENWOOD, SEPT. 25, 1954: Mrs. Harlan Iverson saw a "soaring blue-white ball."

GOLDEN VALLEY, AUG. 3, 1965: Nocturnal light observed.

GOLDEN VALLEY, OCT. 8, 1975: Nocturnal light observed.

GRACEVILLE, SEPT. 25, 1954: The blue-white UFO mentioned above at Glenwood was also sighted here.

GRACEVILLE, NOV. 14, 1956: Marlen Hewitt saw a nocturnal light over U.S. Highway 75.

GRAND MARAIS, SEPT. 5–6, 1966: The UFO discussed at length under the Finland heading was also spotted from this community the same night.

HASTINGS, MARCH 13, 1878: The "mystery airship," or possibly just a meteor, was observed. This period is a little early for the airship wave.

HASTINGS, APRIL 13, 1897: This time it was the airship, seen by someone from Vermillion Street.

HECTOR, APRIL 13, 1897: "Mystery airship."

HERMAN, NOV. 16, 1965: Ray Schuman experienced a close encounter of the first kind.

HERMAN, DEC. 20, 1965: Edward Bruns experienced a close encounter of the second kind.

HIBBING, AUG. 14, 1975: Nocturnal light observed.

INTERNATIONAL FALLS, OCT. 19, 1975: Daylight disc observed.

INTERNATIONAL FALLS, JUNE 28, 1976: Daylight disc observed.

JONESVILLE, APRIL 12, 1897: "Mystery airship."

KINBRAE, APRIL 8, 1965: At 9:30 p.m. a 60-year-old man saw a single bright light in the northwest, about 220 yards away, 33 yards above the ground. It turned east, then left toward the south. It appeared metallic. After a time a door seemed to open in it, and two lights were visible inside. There was radio interference during the sighting.

KINGSTON, DEC. 31, 1977: Kim Cates observed a nocturnal light.

KINGSTON, JULY 3, 1978: Kim Cates again saw a UFO, this time experiencing a close encounter of the second kind.

LAC QUI PARLE LAKE, APRIL 13, 1897: I.J. Monnie observed the "mystery airship."

LAKE CRYSTAL, APRIL 10, 1897: Henry LeClair spotted the "mystery airship."

LAKE ELMO, APRIL 13, 1897: Frederick Chamberlain experienced a close encounter of the third kind.

LAKE LILLIAN, APRIL 13, 1897: "Mystery airship."

LAKE MINNETONKA, JUNE 4, 1963: Nocturnal light observed landing on the lake.

LAKE MINNETONKA, AUG. 3, 1965: Nocturnal light observed.

LA SALLE, NOV. 12, 1969: A deputy sheriff trailed a low-flying nocturnal light.

LENGBY, OCT. 14, 1975: Nocturnal light observed.

LINDSTROM, MARCH 22, 1978: Greg Darr observed nocturnal lights.

LITTLE FALLS, MARCH 23, 1976: Close encounter of the first kind.

LITTLE FORK, FEB. 10, 1976: Close encounter of the first kind.

LONG PRAIRIE, APRIL 20, 1952: Louie Masonick, Jr., observed a daylight disc.

LONG PRAIRIE, OCT. 23, 1965: James Townsend saw the tin-can aliens. See the chapter "Alien in a Can."

LUVERNE, NOV. 15, 1965: UFO observed.

LYLE, 3 a.m. JUNE 4, 1963: Zearl Leinen and four others separately saw a multi-colored object the size of a small truck. Others reported it to be the size of a football field. One woman described it as "a giant Roman candle spouting various colors." It apparently landed. Police on both sides of the Iowa-Minnesota border searched for the object, unsuccessfully.

MADISON LAKE, APRIL 13, 1897: A.M. Haynes saw the "mystery airship."

MANKATO, APRIL 13, 14 AND 19, 1897: The "mystery airship" paid several visits.

MANKATO, 3:53 p.m. NOV. 24, 1951: Air Force pilots W.H. Fairbrother and D.E. Stewart, flying P-51 Mustangs, saw a "milky white" object shaped like a flying wing—a broad, slightly swept-back wing with no fuselage or tail. They estimated the object had an 8-foot span. It flew straight and level and was observed for five seconds. I do not believe it was reported in the media at the time. This sighting was evaluated by the U.S. Air Force's Project Blue Book, which classed it as "unknown."

MCGREGOR, OCT. 21, 1975: Nocturnal light observed.

MEDFORD, NOV. 2, 1975: Close encounter of the second kind. Jane Kay was doing school work at home. Her mother, Helen, was at home. Her brother, Jerry, and his wife were leaving after paying a visit. All described seeing a big orange "ball" lighting on a nearby football field. Jerry at first thought it might be some sort of pyrotechnic device dropped by parachute. After the object departed, soil samples were taken from the site and analyzed by Dr. Edward Zeller of the University of Kansas. The samples showed 10 times the amount of "luminescence" expected. "Exactly what (the results) mean, I can't tell you," Zeller said. "The only thing we can say is that these high variability conditions are unusual."

MEDINA, AUG. 11, 1948: Close encounter of the second kind.

MIDDLE RIVER, DECEMBER 1966: Lorraine Mayone experienced a close encounter of the second kind two miles east of town.

MILLE LACS (LAKE), JAN. 16, 1960: John Hogan observed a strange nocturnal light. Others reported clusters of multi-colored lights.

MINNEAPOLIS, APRIL 10, 1897: "Mystery airship" observed by J.J. Barrett from the Guaranty Loan Restaurant. A day later it was seen by R.G. Adams from 3128 Fourth St.

MINNEAPOLIS, APRIL 13, 1897: "Mystery airship."

MINNEAPOLIS, APRIL 16, 1897: William Cranik spotted the "mystery airship" over Hennepin Avenue.

MINNEAPOLIS, 1938: Harvey L. Sperry observed what later would be termed a daylight disc.

MINNEAPOLIS, JULY 6, 1947: Mrs. Clarence Lasseson experienced a close encounter of the first kind, in the 600 block of West 31st Street.

MINNEAPOLIS, JULY 7, 1947: Dean Ireton spotted a daylight disc over the Omaha Rail Yards. In another incident, a woman saw a glowing, striped object that made a sound like "click-click, phht-phht." The *Minneapolis Star* received 27 local calls reporting UFO sightings this day, so many that they didn't bother to report any of them in detail. Exasperated, columnist Cedric Adams observed, "I, for one, will be glad when the phenomena has been explained."

MINNEAPOLIS, 6:30 a.m. OCT. 11, 1951: Multiple UFO's were seen by General Mills balloon researchers, including aeronautical engineer J.J. Kaliszewski, aerologist C.B. Moore, pilot Dick Reilly in the air, and Doug Smith on the ground. The flight crew saw the first object, a brightly glowing one with a dark underside and a halo around it. The object arrived high and fast, then slowed and made slow climbing circles for about two minutes, and finally sped away to the east. Soon they saw another one, confirmed by ground observers using a tracking instrument, which sped across the sky. Total time the first object was seen was 5 minutes, the second was a few seconds. This sighting was evaluated by the U.S. Air Force's Project Blue Book, which classified it as "unknown." For more information, see the chapter "Cereal Saucers."

MINNEAPOLIS, JUNE 9, 1952: Conspiracy or sloppiness? We know a sighting was made at this place and time because of a dated file folder in the U.S. Air Force's own Project Blue Book files. Whatever this sighting was, the contents of its file have been removed.

The folder's location in the files does indicate that the sighting was evaluated by Project Blue Book, which classified it as "unknown." I believe the sighting was made by astronaut Donald "Deke" Slayton, who was a P-51 fighter pilot at the time. See the chapter "The Astronaut's UFO."

MINNEAPOLIS, OCT. 15, 1953: Staff of the General Mills Aeronautical Research Laboratory observed another daylight disc.

MINNEAPOLIS, MAY 5, 1954: A group of UFOs in "V" formation was observed by astronomy students viewing from the University of Minnesota physics building.

MINNEAPOLIS, JUNE 1, 1954: Beginning at 9 p.m. 400 miles south of the city, the crew of a USAF B-47 jet bomber observed an unknown object with "running lights" for an hour. The plane was flying at 34,000 feet, the UFO at 24,000 to 44,000. This sighting was evaluated by the U.S. Air Force's Project Blue Book, which classified it as "unknown."

MINNEAPOLIS: JUNE 30, 1954: Marvin Tjornhom saw a UFO.

MINNEAPOLIS, SEPT. 25, 1954: A blue-white ball of fire was seen.

MINNEAPOLIS, NOV. 30, 1956: Fred Ewing observed a nocturnal light.

MINNEAPOLIS, DEC. 11, 1956: John Talley observed a nocturnal light.

MINNEAPOLIS, JAN. 1, 1957: R.H. Scrimshaw saw a UFO.

MINNEAPOLIS, AUG. 3, 1965: Nocturnal light observed.

MINNEAPOLIS, OCT. 23, 1965: Ray Blessing observed a nocturnal light.

MINNEAPOLIS, AUG. 16, 1966: Nocturnal light seen from Flying Cloud Airport.

MINNEAPOLIS, FEB. 25, 1967: Joseph E. Sullivan, a photojournalist, saw a nocturnal light from the corner of 1st Avenue and 25th Street.

MINNEAPOLIS, NOV. 26, 1974: Mike Gribovski observed a nocturnal light.

MINNEAPOLIS, OCT. 5, 1975: Close encounter of the first kind.

MINNEAPOLIS, OCT. 19, 1976: Nocturnal light observed near Lake Harriet.

MINNEAPOLIS, FEB. 5, 1977: Rose Strand experienced a close encounter of the first kind.

MINNEAPOLIS, DEC. 12, 1997: A "good-sized red ball" with a tail behind it was seen over four states, including Minnesota, where it was observed by commercial pilots at the Minneapolis-St. Paul International Airport. It was also seen in Wisconsin, Missouri and

Iowa. At La Crescent it was seen about 8 p.m.

MINNETONKA, APRIL 11, 1897: Stuart Mackroth saw the "mystery airship."

MONTGOMERY, APRIL 11, 1897: "Mystery airship."

MOORHEAD, APRIL 26, 1952: Five glowing, circular objects were observed by a police officer and five other adults. The objects were in "V" formation and were flying northwest. In this instance, the Air Force insisted the witnesses had seen ... ground light reflecting off the shiny breasts of ducks.

MOORHEAD, 11:45 p.m. JAN. 17, 1995: A husband and wife and two police officers observed two red lights in the sky. The UFOs were following a small aircraft.

MOTLEY, SEPTEMBER 1969: Sean Blackburn experienced a close encounter of the first kind.

MOUND, OCT. 18, 1973: Bradford Roy spotted a nocturnal light.

MOVIL LAKE, AUGUST 1962: Mildred Anderson experienced a close encounter of the third kind.

MUD LAKE, UNDATED: Glen Miller experienced a close encounter of the third kind.

NEW BRIGHTON, MARCH 22, 1978: Fritz Werdonschegg saw a nocturnal light from Long Lake Road.

NEW LONDON, APRIL 26, 1965: Nine-year-old Gary X. saw an object come down and silently hover about 65 yards away. A periscope, or something like one, then came out of the object. A strange noise was heard (the boy's father heard it, too). After one or two minutes, the periscope went back inside, and the object rose, flying away at unbelievable speed.

NEWFOLDEN, DEC. 18, 1976: Nocturnal light observed.

NEWPORT, OCT. 22, 1954: J.J. Mealy observed a nocturnal light.

NEW SCANDIA, MARCH 22, 1978: Cathy Hawkinson observed nocturnal lights.

NEW ULM, APRIL 19, 1897: The "mystery airship" appeared.

NEW ULM, JUNE 1963: Carl Pfaender saw a daylight disc.

NORWOOD, APRIL 13, 1897: Leopold Henkleman saw the "mystery airship."

OWATONNA, NOVEMBER 1966: Mrs. Ralph Butler experienced a close encounter of the third kind.

PINE RIVER, PROBABLY JANUARY 1968: Close encounter of the third kind.

PRESTON, APRIL 11, 1897: Thomas Wuinn saw the "mystery airship."

RAINY LAKE, MAY 22, 1952: Daylight disc observed.

READING, NOV. 25, 1956: Mary Whelan, age 19, made one of many reports during a 25-day UFO "flap" that had begun Nov. 8 and covered Minnesota and North Dakota. Whelan saw six disc-shaped objects. "They were flying in formation and swished over the farm five or six times," she said. "It was dark. It must have been about 7 o'clock. I was leading my colt around the farmyard to exercise it. All of a sudden the colt became frightened. It stopped and shook its head. Another horse fenced in near the barn acted the same way." Whelan looked up and saw the discs. "They gave off a green light and kept flying in a near semi-circle. They were in the same position every time they flew by."

REGAL, SEPT. 22, 1976: Close encounter of the third kind.

ROCHESTER, MARCH 12, 1967: A boy saw an object that looked like an upside-down mushroom. It was about 11 yards up, and not much larger than a car. It tilted to 45 degrees, oscillated, and then flew away, to the northwest.

ROCHESTER, AUG. 6, 1975: Close encounter of the second kind.

ROCHESTER, OCTOBER 1973: Leroy Martell saw a daylight disc.

ROCHESTER, 3:15 a.m. APRIL 22, 1996: A woman saw a "bright whitish-gold light" hovering in the sky with two smaller objects on each side.

ROCK CREEK, JULY 6, 1947: Carl Dion spotted a daylight disc five miles east of town.

ROSEAU, JULY 1954: UFO observed.

ROSEVILLE, NOV. 16, 1965: Nocturnal light observed.

ROYALTON, APRIL 13, 1897: "Mystery airship" spotted.

SACRED HEART, JAN. 15, 1958: Richard Hoberg experienced a close encounter of the first kind on Highway 212.

ST. ANTHONY, AUG. 3, 1965: Nocturnal light observed.

ST. CLOUD, APRIL 14, 1996: UFO observed. It was described as a large "trapezoid of very bright amber lights with strobes." It passed from the southwest to the northeast. It was also seen in Wisconsin.

ST. GEORGE, 6:10 p.m. OCT. 21, 1965: Deputy Sheriff Arthur A. Strauch and four others observed a nocturnal light two miles northwest of town. Strauch took a color photo of the wedge shaped blob of light, which hovered for five minutes, turning from white to orange and back to white again several times. It then shot off "at a tremendous speed," giving off a high-pitched whine. The sighting was evaluated by the Air Force's Project Blue Book, which classed it as "unknown."

ST. LOUIS PARK, APRIL 28, 1968: Nocturnal light observed.

ST. PAUL, APRIL 11, 1897: The "mystery airship" paid its first visit to the capital, where it was observed by Frank Leavitt, among others.

ST. PAUL, APRIL 13, 1897: James Feeley saw the "mystery airship" from Selby Avenue.

ST. PAUL, OCTOBER 1944: Nellie Carlin had a close encounter of the first kind on the 400 block of Marshall Avenue.

ST. PAUL, JULY 7, 1947: The city had its first sighting of the national wave of UFO reports in 1947. The term "flying saucer" had yet to come into common usage, so the *Pioneer Press* called the objects "whizzits." The paper reported that the first incident happened about 7 p.m. "Speeding west over the busy intersection of Grand and Cleveland was a bright object, about 10 feet in diameter, Robert Doody, 20, 1973 Fairmont Ave., reported." Rita Dawn, walking with Doody, also saw the object. At 10:15 a.m. a "whizzit" was seen by Luther Shaw. It was floating toward Robinsdale at an estimated height of 7,000 feet. Also on this day, "workers at the Omaha railroad yards here swore they observed a disc that resembled the front grill of an automobile." At Wold-Chamberlain Airport at 10:30 p.m., a disc with a long white tail swung slowly overhead. It appeared to be 12 to 15 inches in diameter, flew at about 1,200 feet, and was visible for several minutes before it disappeared in the west. And Olive Erickson, while crossing 33rd Street at 26th Avenue South, saw an airplane pass, followed by something that "looked like a skyrocket and made a yellow glow, although it seemed to be of a red color and was crossed by a white line." The UFO made a "sh-sh-sh" sound. A visually and sonically similar object was also seen this day in Minneapolis. Concurrent with the first sightings was the first ridicule: "Alice M. Car of the Parisian Beauty School, 803 Nicollet Ave., awoke Monday and spotted what she thought was a flying disc. After a tough fight, however, she captured only (a) giant insect. She suggests the insect may be the basis of the flying disc rumors flying around."

ST. PAUL, JULY 8, 1947: Nocturnal light was seen from 625 Grand St. by Laura Behrens.

ST. PAUL, JULY 8, 1952: A rare radar-visual sighting was made by Air Force personnel. Several UFOs were tracked on radar while a pilot tried to intercept fast-moving lights, which sped away.

ST. PAUL, NOV. 14, 1956: Mrs. William O'Keefe observed a nocturnal light.

ST. PAUL, JUNE 4, 1963: Nocturnal light observed.

ST. PAUL, NOV. 26, 1965: Nick DeVara experienced a close encounter of the second kind on Supornick Lane.

ST. PAUL, DEC. 27, 1966: Daylight disc observed.

ST. PAUL, JULY 2, 1975: Nocturnal light observed.

ST. PAUL, APRIL 28, 1978: Daylight disc observed near the corner of George Street and Livingston Avenue.

ST. PETER, NOV. 19, 1976: Nocturnal light observed.

SCANDIA, MARCH 22, 1978: Carol Anderson experienced a close encounter of the first kind on Olinda Trail.

SHAFER, MARCH 22, 1978: Nocturnal light observed by Kari Driver.

SHEVLIN, MAY 15, 1978: Gladys Swanson observed a nocturnal light.

SHOREWOOD, AUG. 3, 1965: Nocturnal light observed.

SIBLEY COUNTY, 10:45 p.m. JUNE 24, 1995: An older woman, alerted by the barking of her dogs, looked and saw "multiple, bizarre, bright colored spheres" floating across her farmyard.

SLEEPY EYE, APRIL 15–16, 1897: On three nights in a row, the "mystery airship" was observed. The first night, witnesses included C. Salkowske; on the second, F. Meilke; on the third, the entire group of Tennessee Jubilee Singers, who had gathered in the town's auditorium.

STARBUCK, SEPT. 10, 1975: Possible ground traces found in association with a close encounter of the second kind.

STEWART, JUNE 24, 1971: Arnold Windschitl found a spot in his cornfield where the green corn had been burned in a 10-foot circle. He'd been awakened earlier by a strange wind, the quacking of ducks and a power failure, all at 12:30 a.m.

STEWARTVILLE, OCT. 24, 1968: Warren Anding had a close encounter of the first kind.

STILLWATER, DEC. 11, 1871: Nocturnal light observed—this is too early a period to be counted as part of the later "mystery airship" flap.

STILLWATER, JAN. 20, 1890: N.A. Nelson saw a nocturnal light—also too early a sighting to be the "mystery airship."

STILLWATER, APRIL 13, 1897: The "mystery airship" is observed.

STILLWATER, AUG. 17, 1961: Five people observed a group of UFOs arranged vertically in a "V" formation.

STILLWATER, JULY 18, 1975: Nocturnal light observed.

STILLWATER, MARCH 22, 1978: Dean Andrie experienced a close encounter of the first kind while traveling north on Highway 95.

SUNRISE, DEC. 2, 1975: Nocturnal light observed.

TAYLORS FALLS, FEB. 6, 1897: "Mystery airship."

THIEF RIVER FALLS, AUGUST 1962: A close encounter of the second kind occurred on U.S. Highway 59.

TOGO, JAN. 3, 1969: Nocturnal light observed.

TWO HARBORS, OCT. 14, 1961: Daylight disc observed over Lake Superior.

TWO HARBORS, APRIL 1, 1975: Close encounter of the first kind.

TWO HARBORS, SEPT. 25, 1975: Nocturnal light observed.

VILLARD, SEPT. 29, 1976: Mrs. Donald Robideaux experienced a close encounter of the first kind.

VIRGINIA, APRIL 12, 1897: The "mystery airship" visited.

VIRGINIA, 10:15 p.m. APRIL 29, 1957: Robert Lerdahl and Alex Ellison saw about three dozen UFOs fly over in groups of six or eight for 40 minutes. They were greenish and appeared through binoculars to be discs traveling in crescent formations. They traveled from east to west, passing from horizon to horizon in eight seconds.

WALKER, AUG. 5, 1966: Nocturnal light observed.

WALKER, AUG. 16, 1966: Jake Miller observed a nocturnal light from Highway 71.

WASECA, APRIL 9, 1897: The "mystery airship" visited.

WASECA, OCT. 13, 1977: Nocturnal light observed.

WASECA, JAN. 22, 1978: Janey Roeglin observed a daylight disc.

WEST BATTLE LAKE, AUG. 16, 1966: Harold Pikal observed a UFO.

WHITE BEAR LAKE, OCT. 17, 1958: Edward Stevens observed a daylight disc.

WINDOM, APRIL 14, 1897: W.A. Peterson observed the "mystery airship."

WINDOM, JUNE 2, 1959: Mrs. Henry X. Buller saw a nocturnal light northeast of town.

WINDOM, NOV. 15, 1965: UFO observed.

WINONA, APRIL 11, 1897: "Mystery airship" observed by Harry Friday and others.

WINONA, NOV. 9, 1965: William Bohn saw a nocturnal light.

WINONA, NOV. 3, 1973: Daylight disc observed over Lake Winona.

WINONA, NOV. 17, 1967: Kenneth Malenke observed a daylight disc.

WINSTED, JAN. 25, 1967: Close encounter of the third kind. A 32-year-old man was driving to work when the engine of his 1964 Chevrolet truck stalled. He got out to check and then saw "an intense light" to his right and approaching. It landed on the road, and the man jumped inside his truck and locked the doors. The UFO had three landing legs and was about 27 feet in diameter and 11 yards high. Something like an elevator descended from the craft, and out came a figure in blue overalls, "with something like a fishbowl on his head." The figure seemed to check something, returned to its craft, and left.

WOODSIDE TOWNSHIP, MID-NOVEMBER 1965: Close encounter of the second kind.

WYOMING, 2:10 a.m. APRIL 14, 1996: A man and his three neighbors saw a "huge" cluster of lights pass from the southwest to northeast. It moved at a steady pace and made no noise. The sky was clear.

YOUNG AMERICA, APRIL 13, 1897: "Mystery airship."

MINNESOTA-WISCONSIN BORDER, JULY 28, 1952: Air Force jets chased a UFO tracked by ground radar. The UFOs sped away from the interceptors. The objects' speeds ranged from 60 to 600 m.p.h.

MINNESOTA-WISCONSIN BORDER, NIGHT OF NOV. 26, 1965: This was a night of power failures for residents on both sides of the border. Beginning shortly after 8 p.m. an object with blinking blue lights was seen in and around St. Paul, Minn. It sent out occasional flashes of bright blue light. The UFO was observed by many, including police officers in Totem Town, Minn., who reported to the Northern States Power Co. that the power failures plaguing the utility's customers that night coincided with the object's appearance. The utility could not explain the outages. See the chapter "Blackout!"

MINNESOTA-WISCONSIN BORDER, FROM 8:45 TO 9:15 p.m. MARCH 22, 1978: Dozens of witnesses reported a nocturnal light traveling roughly on a path from Cumberland, Barron County, Wis., to St. Paul, Minn.

SOUTHEASTERN MINNESOTA, FEB. 15, 1963: A bright, fast-moving UFO was seen by many as it flew to the northeast.

THE ASTRONAUT'S UFO

In January 1974, Don Berliner, of the Fund for UFO Research, a civilian investigative group, visited the U.S. Air Force Archives at Max-well Air Force Base in Montgomery, Ala., to review the files of Pro-ject Blue Book.

Project Blue Book was the U.S. Air Force's own UFO investigation unit from 1952 until 1969, when it was officially closed. Earlier, Project Sign and Project Grudge had been the Air Force's UFO units (yes, the significance of the formerly secret name "Grudge" has been noted by many); each of the three UFO projects was based at the Air-Technical Intelligence Center at Wright-Patterson Air Force Base in Dayton, Ohio, and each succeeding project incorporated the earlier unit's files into its own. Thus, Project Blue Book's archived records also contain the records for Sign and Grudge.

While Berliner never published the book for which he conducted the research, he has made his notes available to other investigators.

"In a full week, I read all the 'unexplained' cases in the original files and made extensive notes, including the names and other identifying information on all witnesses where given," he said. "The cooperation of the staff of the archives was excellent, and no restrictions were placed on my work."

A few months later, however, the files were withdrawn from public view so they could be prepared for transfer to the National Archives in Washington, D.C. The 30 file drawers of material, more than 12,000 case files, were photocopied. Names and other identifying information were blacked out, and the censored photocopies were microfilmed. Only this microfilm is today available to researchers; the original files, still held by the National Archives, are unavailable.

The censorship was aggressive, extending even to names in newspaper clippings contained in the files.

Even more disturbing, before Berliner got to look at the original information during his January 1974 visit, material contained in 13 file folders had been removed—lost or stolen. While several of Project Blue Book's own personnel decried the state of its files over the years, during the period we are now going to look at, the operation was fairly well organized. This is according to Capt. Edward Ruppelt, a frank and free-thinking man who headed Blue Book from 1952 to 1954.

One of the 13 missing files is from Minneapolis, June 9, 1952. The dated file folder remained, but its contents were gone. While we don't know what happened to the material, the folder's location in the files does indicate that the sighting was evaluated by the Air Force, which classified it as "unknown." I believe I know what the sighting was: a sighting made by a man who would later become an astronaut—an absolutely embarrassing predicament for the Air Force, which had for so long tried to discount UFO reports.

The sighting was made by Donald "Deke" Slayton. A Wisconsin native, Slayton enlisted in the U.S. Air Force during World War II and received his pilot's wings in 1943. He flew 56 combat missions over Europe as a member of the 340th Bombardment Group, and then went on to fly seven missions over Japan. After the war he completed a Bachelor of Science degree in aeronautical engineering at the University of Minnesota and found employment at the Boeing Aircraft Corp. in Seattle. He was recalled to active duty in 1951, and Slayton served as a flight test officer, technical inspector, fighter pilot and experimental test pilot until April 1959, when he was named one of NASA's original seven Mercury astronauts.

In September 1962, Slayton was made the first chief of NASA's Astronaut Office and then director of Flight Crew Operations. He was the docking pilot for the July 1975 Apollo/Soyuz rendezvous. He later worked on development of the space shuttle.

Slayton recalled the UFO incident almost 20 years later as occurring in 1951, but I believe he was in error, and that the sighting actually happened in 1952. In 1951 Slayton was made a maintenance officer and test pilot for a P-51 fighter group based in Minneapolis. While flight-testing one of the aircraft in bright daylight, he encountered a disc-shaped object and pursued it.

As Slayton later wrote to UFO researcher Dr. J. Allen Hynek:

"I was cruising at about 10,000 feet. The only reason this number sticks in my mind is because my first reaction upon seeing the object was that it was a kite, and a few seconds later it occurred to me that this could not be the case (because of the altitude).

"Upon closer examination the object was obviously at about my altitude and seemed to be coming from the opposite direction, so I continued to watch it until it was directly off my left wing and about 500 feet below. At this point it appeared to be a round balloon of about the size of a weather balloon, and I assumed that was what it was. I decided to make a pass on it and did a 180-degree turn, which put me directly in trail of the object.

"Upon getting in trail, it appeared to be a disc-shaped object rather than round, sitting at about a 45-degree angle with the horizon. The object seemed somewhat slower than I at that point, but started to accelerate and went into a climbing left turn as I closed on it. I lost sight of it ... and returned to home base. I did make a report the following day to our intelligence section ...."

Trying to downplay the sighting, Slayton wrote Hynek that he did not attach great importance to it. "My only conclusion was that it was an unidentified object, at least to me, and I would not speculate as to what it might have been," he said. "Since it was a bright, clear day, I have discounted its being a weather illusion or an optical illusion."

CEREAL SAUCERS

I n 1952 the Air Force came to Minneapolis for help. The government was reorganizing its investigation into the UFO problem. In charge was Capt. Edward J. Ruppelt, a fresh officer with new ideas—even the secret name of the project was going to be changed, from Project Grudge to Blue Book, in reference to the university copybooks into which students write the answers to hard questions.

Ruppelt came to town with a scientist from an Ohio-based private think tank, the Battelle Memorial Institute, which had been tapped by the Air Force to help make sense of UFO sightings. The two were coming to see scientists at, of all places, General Mills.

"The Aeronautical Division of General Mills, Inc., of Wheaties and Betty Crocker fame, had launched and tracked every (weather) balloon that had been launched prior to mid-1952," Ruppelt explained in his classic book, *The Report on Unidentified Flying Saucers*. Weather balloons had been frequently blamed for UFO sightings. General Mills is a large, diversified company, but why its interests included (or still include) an aeronautical division with military contracts is apparently a secret—the company did not return my calls. But the company was and perhaps is tops in aeronautics, with no competing government contractors.

"They knew what their balloons looked like under all lighting conditions and they also knew meteorology, aerodynamics, astronomy, and they also knew UFOs," Ruppelt said. The scientists had just begun sending in reports of what they'd seen because they'd heard of the Air Force reorganization.

"They, like so many other reliable observers, had been disgusted with the previous Air Force attitude toward UFO reports, and they had refused to send in any reports. I decided that these people might be a good source of information, and I wanted to get further details on their reports, so I got orders to go to Minneapolis," Ruppelt added.

He and the Battelle scientist arrived on Jan. 14, 1952, in the middle of a snowstorm. "I talked to these people for the better part of a full day," Ruppelt said, "and every time I tried to infer that there might be some natural explanation for the UFOs, I just about found myself in a fresh snowdrift."

What made the General Mills staff so sure of the UFO reality? "In the first place, they had seen so many of them," Ruppelt said. "One man told me that one tracking crew had seen so many that the sight of a UFO no longer even especially interested them. And the things that they saw couldn't be explained."

Many of the General Mills' reports came from other parts of the country where the company's aeronautical research had been conducted, especially New Mexico.

The first of the Twin Cities' sightings reported to the Air Force by the astonishingly qualified General Mills scientists came on Oct. 10, 1951. J.J. Kaliszewski, who was the supervisor of balloon manufacture at the General Mills Aeronautical Research Laboratories, was flying with Jack Donaghue north of Minneapolis at an altitude of 4,000 feet, tracking a "skyhook"-type balloon.

"We started a climb towards the balloon on a course of 230 degrees," Kaliszewski later wrote. "At 6,000 feet I noticed a strange object crossing the skies from east to west, a great deal higher and behind our balloon."

The balloon was about 20,000 feet. The object appeared to be a quarter the size of the balloon, six miles northeast of it.

"The object had a peculiar glow to it," Kaliszewski recalled. It crossed behind and above the balloon from east to west very rapidly, first coming in at a slight dive, leveling off for a minute and then slowing. Then it went into a sharp left turn, climbed at 50 or 60 degrees into the southeast "with terrific acceleration" and disappeared.

"Jack Donaghue and I observed this object for about two minutes and it crossed through an arc of approximately 40 degrees to 50 degrees. We saw no vapor trail, and from past experience I know that the object was not a balloon, jet, conventional aircraft or celestial star."

The next day Kaliszewski was in the air again, this time with Dick Reilly. They were observing a "grab bag" balloon, flying at 10,000 feet, when they saw a brightly glowing object to the southeast of the University of Minnesota airport.

"The object was moving from east to west at a high rate and very high," Kaliszewski wrote. They kept the plane on a constant course and used a reinforcement on the windshield as a marker to track the object's movement. It moved at 5 degrees per second.

"This object was peculiar in that it had what can be described as a halo around it with a dark under-surface," Kaliszewski wrote. "It crossed rapidly and then slowed down and started to climb in lazy circles slowly. The pattern it made was like a falling oak leaf inverted. It went through these gyrations for a couple of minutes."

Kaliszewski called his tracking station at the airport, which spotted several similar UFOs in the vicinity, but the objects moved so quickly that measurements could not be taken. Kaliszewski and Reilly's own sighting lasted about five minutes. Two hours later they saw another, but it quickly left, arriving from the west and departing to the east.

On Oct. 15, 1953, three research engineers at the General Mills Aeronautical Laboratories saw another UFO. It was 10:10 a.m. They were tracking a 79-foot balloon floating at about 80,000 feet.

At first the UFO itself wasn't visible, but it was leaving a visible vapor trail, which quickly disappeared. It passed beneath the sun at an elevation of about 25 degrees, heading south on a horizontal course. It was moving at a rate of 10 degrees per 9 seconds. The altitude was estimated at 40,000—for a speed of 15 miles per minute or 900 miles per hour. But all the witnesses agreed that the object's estimated altitude might have been as much as 60,000 feet—for a speed of 1,200 miles per hour.

After about 10 seconds, the object went into a vertical dive without changing its speed. That lasted for 10 to 15 seconds, and the object was finally visible two or three times as it glowed or reflected the sunlight momentarily. Then the trail of vapor or smoke stopped, and there was the object itself—not glowing, not glaring; it was a gray mass, just leveling off. Its size in the optical tracking equipment was about that of the balloon, and since the UFO appeared nearer than the balloon, the UFO must have been smaller than the balloon's 79-foot diameter.

Asked what a "most likely" explanation could be, the witnesses said it could have been a jet aircraft. But they made four points:

1) The speed was higher than would normally be observed—perhaps much greater.
2) The vertical dive was dangerous if not suicidal.
3) A jet making such a dive would be heard for miles and would certainly cause a noticeable shock wave beneath it.
4) Vapor trails do not ordinarily occur during vertical motion, though a smoke trail might.

Astronomer J. Allen Hynek was at the time a special advisor to Ruppelt's Air Force UFO investigative unit, Project Blue Book. Hynek later recalled, "Well, even Blue Book evaluated this as 'Unidentified.' Perhaps the suicidal dive was too much for them."

More likely, it was the extreme competence of the General Mills' scientists who worked daily with the balloons under all lighting and weather conditions.

For his part, Ruppelt recalled that "after my visit to General Mills, Inc., I couldn't help remembering a magazine article I'd read a year before. It said that there was not a single reliable UFO report that couldn't be attributed to a skyhook balloon." But the balloon experts themselves had disagreed.

BLACKOUT!

Aclose encounter of the second kind, as we have already noted, is an incident in which a UFO somehow interacts with the environment. It may leave landing marks, avoid a passing aircraft, or in some other way show that it is more than a mirage.

You may have had a close encounter of the second kind and not even known it.

In 1960, a civilian research group, the National Investigations Committee on Aerial Phenomena (NICAP), published a brochure on an attribute of flying saucers that had been suspected but never before been fully analyzed: the disruption of electromagnetic fields. The effects noted in association with the appearance of UFOs included radio and television interference, stalled autos, stopped wristwatches and even blackouts of communities.

The earliest reported case of the UFO's electromagnetic effect occurred on Aug. 28, 1945, when a military plane near Iwo Jima had engine trouble and lost altitude as three UFOs flew nearby. NICAP found 112 similar cases of electromagnetic effect between 1945 and 1960.

Why a UFO would have such an effect is of course unknown. It could be that a UFO somehow drains power from systems. Some have suggested that a UFO powered by nuclear energy may emit the same sort of electromagnetic pulse characteristic of nuclear explosions—which similarly disrupt electromagnetic fields.

Because the reported movements of UFOs often seem to operate without regard to inertia—90-degree turns without slowing, for example—most UFO theorists believe that the objects are somehow able to manipulate gravity. A UFO likely cancels out existing gravity and operates within its own gravity field. Whatever the power source, an electromagnetic field is cast around the craft. One benefit is that it would require little energy to propel the craft, since it would be gravity-neutral. Such an electromagnetic field would be expected to glow and change color, depending on the craft's movement—just as is often reported in sightings of UFOs. Such a field would also have caused strange events in and around the Twin Cities on Nov. 27, 1965.

It had been, in retrospect, a strange week, at least for readers of the *Minneapolis Morning Tribune*. It almost seemed as if the public was being prepared for an alien encounter. On the 22nd the newspaper had run a painting of a bulbous-headed alien, accompanying a special article by Isaac Asimov on the nature of life in the universe. On the 25th appeared an editorial cartoon showing the earth with two rings of man-made satellites, forming two halos. The caption read, "Beginning to look like Saturn."

On the 27th the *Minneapolis Morning Tribune* ran a feature article headlined, "Life in other worlds could shake our beliefs." It was buried on an inside page. The top story was the snowstorm of the night before—14 inches!—and the power failures that had blacked out St. Paul and neighboring areas. The reporter hadn't checked with the utilities, but he or she blamed the storm.

The *Pioneer Press* did check. The Northern States Power Co. could not explain the blackout. Nothing had gone wrong. Yet everything did.

The *Pioneer Press* reported that power had failed in and around the city while, at the same time, one or more UFOs were observed. Just after 8 p.m. witnesses watched an object with blinking blue lights send down flashes of brighter blue light, like the spurt of a welding torch. As it passed, Nick DeVara and Mark Wilcox saw a brightly lit service station black out. When the UFO left, the station lit up again. It moved north, and when it appeared over Hogt Avenue, a witness reported, the "blue glowing" object seemed to make power fail throughout the area. A motorist even reported that his car lights and radio had gone out.

In Totem Town, on Highway 61 near St. Paul, a pair of UFOs crossed overhead at low altitude, giving off blue and orange flashes. Several police officers were among the observers who reported to the Northern States Power Co. that as soon as the UFOs appeared, all electric power failed.

Similar sightings had taken place earlier in the month. On the night of Nov. 9, Robert C. Walsh, Deputy City Aviation Commissioner for Syracuse, N.Y., had been flying over that city at about 1,500 feet when every light beneath him went out. "I thought of sabotage. I thought of a lot of things," he later said. He landed and got out of his plane, looked up and saw a great ball of light. "It appeared to be about 100 feet in the air and 50 feet in diameter," he said. Several similar objects were photographed from St. Paul's Episcopal Church. The fireball, or something similar to it, was also seen outside the city by Renato Pacini, assistant conductor of the Indianapolis Symphony Orchestra. At Niagara Falls, a flight instructor and his student, Weldon Ross and James Brooking, respectively, watched from the air as a red globe hovered over power lines leading to the Falls' generating plant.

That same night New York City was also blacked out—and *Time* magazine later ran a photo of the dark skyline with a spindle-shaped object overhead. The caption asked, "Could this be a UFO?" Similar objects were seen in Philadelphia, West Orange, N.J., and Bloomfield, Conn.

This was the 1965 Northeast Power Grid blackout, which plunged a fifth of the nation, 36 million people, into darkness. Two months later the *New York Times* reported that the source of the power loss still had not been found. Unexplainable blackouts also took place Dec. 2 at Juarez, Mexico, Las Cruces and Alamogordo, N.M., and El Paso, Texas; and on Dec. 26 in Argentina and Finland.

It would seem that all the residents of these areas were participants in far-flung close encounters of the second kind.

WHEN PROPHECY COMES TRUE

A bunch of flying saucer nuts receive psychic messages from outer space, warning of the end of the world. They are a mixed crowd of professionals, students and housewives. Their mysterious communications come from an astral body masked by a huge, fiery object within our own solar system. Thankfully—so they believe—UFOs will land just beforehand to gather the faithful. All others—the sinful, the disbelieving—will perish.

The prophesied date of destruction arrives—passes—and the world does not end—except for the personal worlds of the group's members.

This is not a story set in Rancho Santa Fe, Calif., but in Minnesota. Rancho Santa Fe is where admitted alien and self-trained guru Marshall Herff Applewhite led 38 members of his Heaven's Gate cult to join him in committing suicide in 1997. Their purpose: body-and-soul transmigration to the UFO supposedly hidden behind comet Hale-Bopp, which at the time was speeding toward earth. You probably remember seeing the news photos of the members' bodies, all laid out neatly in the bunks of their pricey mansion.

The dynamics of end-of-the-world cults have been fairly well understood for four decades. In 1956 the classic sociological study on such groups was released: *When Prophecy Fails*. The book was written by a team of researchers working with the Laboratory for Research in Social Relations at the University of Minnesota. It tells the sad story of a group of men and women from Lake City and Collegeville.*

For the purposes of the study, the university researchers penetrated the group and gave the inside story of the tragic pseudo-religious movement. Not for a moment did the writers consider that the saucer-buffs might be experiencing something real; none of the members' experiences were taken within the context of the larger, more mainstream study of unidentified flying objects. In fact, the writers ignored many very real UFO reports recorded throughout the area during the course of their study.

Even after studying the story in depth, one finds it hard to disagree with the university folk; the saucer buffs were sadly fooling themselves. And yet the group might, after all, have been experiencing *something* that was real.

The scholarly perspective slammed the group—not much of a challenge to make fun of flying saucer buffs. In the interest of equal time, in this chapter I'll argue in favor of those Lake City citizens who believed—and continued to believe after the world did not end.

One day in 1954 from out of Lake City came a news story headlined "PROPHECY FROM PLANET CLARION, CALL TO CITY: FLEE THAT FLOOD, IT'LL SWAMP US ON DEC. 21 ...."

The story said that Lake City would be destroyed, apparently by a flood from Lake Pepin, just before dawn, Dec. 21, according to Mrs. Marian Keech, 707 S. Cuyler Ave., who had received the warning in trance, as a spirit medium, or go-between. She got the messages through automatic writing—a phenomenon in which a person's will is turned over to the soul of another, who then uses the earthly body to pen communications.

"The messages, according to Mrs. Keech, are sent to her by superior beings from a planet called 'Clarion.' These beings have been visiting the earth, she says, in what we call flying saucers," said the news story.

"During their visits, she says, they have observed fault lines in the earth's crust that foretoken the deluge. Mrs. Keech reports she was

---

* Out of respect to the group, the university sociologists gave the group's members fictitious names and changed the locales; while I know the real names and places, for convenience to those familiar with *When Prophecy Fails,* and to continue to preserve anonymity, I extend the authors' practice to the new material I am adding to the story. Thus, when I write of Lake City or Collegeville, even when reporting new information, I am referring to the actual communities where the events took place.

told the flood will spread to form an inland sea stretching from the Arctic Circle to the Gulf of Mexico. At the same time, she says, a cataclysm will submerge the West Coast from Seattle, Wash., to Chile in South America."

I hope I'm not giving the ending away here when I tell you that the world, or even pastoral Lake City, did not come to an end. But I'd like to remind you that, at the time, such a holocaust seemed much more possible than now. This was a very dynamic period in American history. The so-called Lake City Group did not arise from a vacuum.

In 1953 a warning of similar Biblical proportions had been received: "The atomic secret is the fruit of your sick imaginations: Science develops everywhere at the same rhythm, and the manufacture of bombs is a mere matter of industrial capabilities. You have simply tried to halt the progress of science by human sacrifice—we are here getting the point: Your country is sick with fear."

The message was not from outer space. It was an open letter to Americans from Jean-Paul Sartre regarding Julius and Ethel Rosenberg, who were executed for allegedly giving nuclear secrets to the Soviets. In the same year, an armistice stopped the Korean War. The first hydrogen bomb was a year away, as were the Army-McCarthy hearings; as was the Supreme Court's ruling on *Brown vs. Board of Ed-ucation,* striking down "separate but equal" facilities; as was the attempted assassination on the floor of Congress of five U.S. Repre-sentatives by Puerto Rican nationalists. Another year later and "Rock Around the Clock" became a hit; Rosa Parks refused to give up her seat on a Montgomery, Ala., bus; and Bishop Fulton Sheen announced, "The communist loves nothing better than to be arrested. But he is not like the martyr for the faith. St. Joan of Arc did not like being tied to a stake; a communist does."

Another woman who heard voices, as did St. Joan of Arc, was Mrs. Marian Keech, our Minnesota flying saucer medium. In her own way, she would be as severely tested, in times which were arguably just as tempestuous.

It began early one winter morning when Marian Keech woke up and felt a tingling in her arm all the way up to her shoulder.

"I had the feeling that someone was trying to get my attention," she said. "Without knowing why, I picked up a pencil and a pad that were lying on the table near my bed. My hand began to write in another handwriting."

The handwriting looked familiar to Keech, and yet it was not her own. She said, "Will you identify yourself?" And the answer came from her own hand: it was her dead father.

This is called automatic writing and is a form of mediumship. It has been known since the middle of the 19th century, when spiritualism became something of a fad. There were, and are, many methods of spirit communication. Spiritualism researchers determined that the various phenomena manifested according to the abilities of each specific human medium. Some mediums were able to channel voices. Others produced ectoplasm—phantom images of the deceased, who could walk, talk and handle objects. Some mediums were able to have their spirit contacts write for themselves, and those ghosts moved chalk over blackboards without any human assistance. Other mediums had to actually do the writing themselves—not dictation, exactly, so much as giving their hands over to the spirits. Still others hadn't even that facility, but had to recite the alphabet and wait for spirit "raps" to interrupt, laboriously spelling out sentences a letter at a time.

Even in the more spiritually sympathetic time of a century ago, none of this activity was seen as especially reliable. Sir Arthur Conan Doyle, creator of Sherlock Holmes and probably the most famous and dedicated of late 19th and early 20th century spiritualist investigators, concluded that, "Unhappily, (automatic writing) is a method which lends itself very readily to self-deception, since it is certain that the subconscious mind of man has many powers with which we are as yet imperfectly acquainted. It is impossible ever to accept any automatic script wholeheartedly as a hundred percent statement of truth from the Beyond. The stained glass will still tint that light which passes through it, and our human organism will never be crystal clear."

Doyle made another point, which I have updated for students in classes on unexplained phenomena, which I teach: with a seance or Ouija board or other attempt at spirit communication, you are essentially placing a prank call to heaven. You're dialing a number at random. Just because you get somebody on the line, it doesn't mean they are balanced or sensitive, or are truthful or have the gift of pro-phecy. They might even be rude and (no pun intended) mean-spirited. They might lie or have fun messing with your mind. You don't have to be nice to be dead.

At any rate, Marian Keech recognized that her own ability was elementary, and she worked to develop her automatic writing skills.

Her early attempts were halting and contained strange words. But she produced a letter from her father to her mother. Dad was worried about spring flower planting, it seemed. Marian's mother didn't really appreciate the message.

One interesting note is that at this point Marian became aware there were souls other than her father's who were trying to "get through" to her.

"It occurred to me that if my father could use my hand, Higher Forces could (also) use my hand," Marian later told the university's undercover investigators. She did have an awareness that not all the spirits might be good. "I don't mind telling you I prayed very diligently that I would not fall into the wrong hands."

As it turned out, she probably did—if we accept this model of the afterlife, which the university people of course did not. But this is one possible alternative explanation. Marian really was communicating with spirits. They just weren't very nice.

But they seemed helpful enough, especially at first. Marian's first new friend on the other end of the line identified him/her/itself as "the Elder Brother." Elder Brother said that Marian's father was in need of considerable spiritual instruction so that he could advance to a higher state. (This, again, is classic spiritualism; many earlier mediums, in fact, had taken it upon themselves to conduct a sort of spiritual missionary work, helping confused souls move on.) The Elder Brother and Marian tried to help her father, but Dad didn't really take to it. The Elder Brother gave up, and told Marian that she might want to work on her own spiritual development instead.

At this point, Marian moved outside everything that had been established under Victorian spiritualism.

Spiritualism, by itself, requires many assumptions which even its practitioners seldom consider. They are: that the person has an imperishable something, such as a soul; that this soul can, at least sometimes, survive bodily death; that the energy of the soul maintains its coherence and is not merely dissipated; that it has the power of communication (by definition, in this case, extrasensory communication); and that certain human adepts also enjoy this talent in life and are thus able to bridge the gap between living and dead.

To all this Marian added four new assumptions: that there is life on other planets; that these life forms exist in continuity with what humans perceive of as an afterlife—Mars is heaven, perhaps; that the raw stuff that makes up ESP is universally constant—that a Martian's concept of the color red, for example, is identical to our own, and is not so hopelessly different as to be unrecognizable and beyond translation; and that therefore the aliens may be communicated with as easily as the human dead.

At the time, of course, Marian didn't think it all through that clearly. In fact, she probably never did. All Marian knew was that she was receiving writings from new spirit beings who claimed to live on the planets Clarion and Cerus.

Clarion is a "planet" well-known to UFO researchers, though the university people didn't pick up on that. That's the first of their major oversights. Clarion is not made up—or at least Marian didn't make it up. It's something of a mystery in itself how she heard about it.

Clarion supposedly is a planet within our own solar system. As a matter of fact, it's in the same orbit as earth. But it's always on the opposite side of the sun, so we never see it. Word of its supposed presence was first revealed by Truman Bethurum in 1954. He was a construction worker who'd been laying asphalt in the Mojave Desert when he encountered a flying saucer. It was captained by a beautiful and lovely alien named Aura Rhanes. A native of Clarion, she described itas a place without war. Even better, there was no divorce or taxes.

Bethurum was one of several of the "contactees" who claimed alien meetings in the 1950s, and who all but disgraced serious investigation of UFOs. But it is interesting that his account of the meeting, *Aboard a Flying Saucer,* did not appear until 1954. Within the first three months of that year—possibly earlier—Marian Keech had claimed her own contact with Clarion. She either bought Bethurum's book as soon as it came out (I'm uncertain as to when in 1954 it appeared), or she and Bethurum had contact, or she and Bethurum came up with the planet's name independently.

I don't think it is a coincidence that at this point, April 8, Larry W. Bryant saw a UFO over Lake City's yacht club. On the same day at 4 p.m., Lelah H. Stoker watched while over the lake a white, round-topped disc, with a humanoid somehow suspended beneath it, flew over the lake. According to Stoker, the disc landed, and yet another occupant apparently got out and walked around. It wore a green suit. The occupant returned to the disc, and it took off very, very fast. The entire sighting lasted about 30 minutes. The incident was later investigated by the U.S. Air Force's UFO investigative unit, Project Blue

Book, which did not write it off as a hoax or lie, as it so often did in similar cases. Instead, this close encounter of the third kind was evaluated as "unknown."

Both these sightings were undoubtedly the talk of the town. And yet they were ignored by the university researchers.

In mid-April Marian began receiving messages from Sananda. Sananda later revealed himself to be Jesus Christ, and indicated he was looking for new disciples. A few days after Easter, one of Sananda's assistants wrote to Marian, "What can you do for us? Well, you can go tell the world that we have at last contacted the Earth planet with the waves of ether that have become tactable by the bombs your scientists have been exploding."

Mmm hmm.

Fortunately, as Christ so often did when explaining complex philosophical matters to his followers, the speaker clarified the ether-tactable process by rendering it as an analogy. He wrote, "This works like an accordion."

If that explanation were not clear enough: "When the condensation leaves the carceious level of the ether or atmosphere levels that support a large light layer of marine life, it causes a barrier to be set up. Now that the bombs have broken that layer we can break through. That is what your scientists call the sonic barrier." (Actually, it isn't.) "We have been trying to get through for many of your years, with alce-topes and the earling timer."

Don't worry. We'll get to definitions in a minute. At about this time, June 8, another UFO was observed over Lake City. It also was ignored by the university researchers.

Sananda later advised Marian to get some "real level-thinking people around you. Get a couple of learned friends that can stabilize you. Let them know what you are doing."

Marian talked to her husband about it. He was a traffic manager at a distributing company. The university researchers noted that he was "a man of infinite patience, gentleness, and tolerance amounting almost to self-abasement." He never believed his wife, but he never opposed her activities.

Marian then told a woman acquaintance about the messages; two of the acquaintance's friends in turn learned about Marian. An informal group began meeting to discuss the messages.

As luck would have it, a flying saucer lecturer then visited Lake

City—his name was not recorded, but was it Truman Bethurum, I wonder? Marian saw his presentation and shared news of her activities with him. He continued on to Collegeville, where he told Dr. Thomas Armstrong. Dr. Armstrong at that time did not know Marian, but he was to become her strongest proponent.

Armstrong and his wife, Daisy, hailed from Kansas. They had worked as medical missionaries in Egypt. In Collegeville he chaired a religious study group under the auspices of a nondenominational church. This group was called The Seekers. The Armstrongs got in touch with Marian, and Sananda/Jesus himself told Marian, "Go to Collegeville." So she did.

They became friends, and corresponded—by mail. Through other means, Marian was now receiving as many as 10 spirit messages a day. Some were just a sentence or two, though most were 250 words. From these teachings came a revelatory portrait of the universe's workings. This is it:

There are other life forms in the universe. Some have superior wisdom. They bear some resemblance to humans, but exist at a higher "vibratory frequency" than humans.*

Many, many, many years ago, the planet Car was divided. On one side were "the scientists," led by Lucifer. On the other side were "the people who followed the light." The scientists threatened to destroy the light, and nearly did destroy the planet, through their foolish use of alcetopes. This caused a disturbance in the omniverse, of course. The forces of light fled to the planets Clarion, Cerus and Uranus. Lucifer and his bunch came to Earth. He and his scientists still work here to destroy good. A while ago, Clarion sent Jesus over. He was partly successful. But Lucifer and his folks are getting pretty strong and it will come to a head soon.

In fact—but wait a moment. I beg the reader's pardon while I digress to define some terms:

Avagada—space ship, operating on "light force propulsion."

Celecoblet—"something your scientists have not yet imagined," but which transmits thoughts as magnetic energy.

Inter-conscious-perception—ESP.

Lear—the earthling's body.

---

*In contemporary scientific jargon, we'd say that these life forms inhabit a parallel universe, overlaid upon our own; this, in fact, is a cutting-edge hypothesis attempting to explain the alien abduction phenomenon; and in a rough way, a parallel universe's necessarily different rate of atomic vibration would make some sense of the "sonic barrier" referred on page 68.

Losolo—school of the universe.

Omniverse—the larger overall universe of universes.

Sibet—student.

Thermin—thought and action recorder.

UN—intelligence of the Creator; mind of the high self.

(These aren't all nonsense terms, at least not entirely. There is no such thing as an alcetope, though that could possibly be interpreted as a compound acting as an "alcahest," the universal solvent long sought by alchemists. The idea of a solvent to get through a barrier, "sonic" or not, is intriguing.)

Anyway, the good side has the Creator, and the Creator has the UN, and the UN has Guardians. The Guardians create the avagadas. It hardly seems necessary to create an avagada, given the wonderful thermin, and the use we are able to make of it with the celecoblet. So it must be that it is pleasing for a Guardian to have an avagada or two.

The Guardians are obviously at a very high state of spiritual evolution. They never go back to the lear. In fact, they do not know death. Which is not to say that life on Clarion is all pleasant. "We have weather—snow and rain," admitted Sananda.

One of the things Guardians do for fun is teach those of us who are still in our lears. That's part of the Losolo—sort of university extension work. As a matter of fact, "it is the ignorance of the Universal Laws that makes all the misery of the Earth," and "We see and know that you struggle in darkness and want to bring real light, for yours is the only planet that has war and hatred.

"We feel no sadness but are interested in the progress of the people of your Earth. Why? We are all brothers. Need I tell you more?"

This is all harmless and actually fairly pleasant stuff. It boils down to, "Be nice." Other flying saucer contactees had received similar messages. Sananda and Elder Brother also explained that they had started to have real physical contact with the Earth people. In fact, "We are trying to make arrangements for a party of six from Westing-house to visit your world with us."

Finally, Sananda admitted, there was an urgency to his teachings. Lucifer would soon be ready for war. "We are planning to come in great numbers in the weeks ahead, as the war preparations are being formulated ... (certain earth dwellers) will be gathered up and relieved of the experiences of the holocaust of the coming events."

On July 23, Marian was told by Sananda to go to a nearby airfield.

A flying saucer would land there at noon on a certain day. "It is a very accurate cast that we give," wrote Sananda. She invited the Armstrongs to witness the event, and they and nine others parked on a sleepy road bordering the airfield.

"We didn't know what we were looking for," said Marian later. "We were looking for saucers. As we stood eating our lunch from the back of the car, just standing out in the fields alongside the road ...."

The road was long and straight. But suddenly Marian noticed a man approaching. They hadn't seen him before. As he came near she had a strange feeling. One of the other women said, "Be careful, that man is crazy." Marian offered him a sandwich and a glass of juice. He said no.

"I couldn't imagine anybody that time of day on a lonely highway not wanting a cold drink," Marian recalled. "I asked him again, but he said: 'No, thank you.' I looked at his eyes—eyes that looked through my soul—and the words sent electric currents to my feet."

As they all stood there looking up for flying saucers, the man looked up, too—and then looked at the party, "at me especially," said Marian.

I don't doubt it.

Finally the man walked off. When he was maybe 20 feet distant, Marian turned away momentarily, and when she looked back he was gone. He'd just disappeared!

No saucers came and after two hours everyone left. But soon came the wonderful spirit-written news.

"It was I, Sananda, who appeared on the roadside in the guise of the sice." Jesus had come to Lake City.

Here was another new word—"sice." From its context, Marian took it to be "one who comes in disguise." The university researchers believed it to be a nonsense word, and added a long footnote noting its earlier use in another of Marian's more bizarre communications. However, both Marian and the researchers were wrong. It's a real word. It's Urdu for servant, or groomsman. It's a bit obscure, but you can find it in the works of Rudyard Kipling. The reality of this term is especially disturbing to me, and is what has spurred me to take the Lake City group's experiences at least half seriously. It suggests that Marian may have entertained an angel, unaware.

Still, disappointed in flying saucers that were not punctual, some of the group drifted away. Those who remained hardened in their faith and new converts were added from Dr. Armstrong's religious study group, The Seekers. Soon Marian traveled to stay with the Armstrongs, where she received more detailed descriptions from Sananda of the end of the world. This time he gave the date—Dec. 21.

"And the scenes of the day will be as mad. The grosser ones (those with denser souls) will be as mad. And the ones of the light will be as the sibets (students) of teachers who have drilled them for this day."

The Rocky Mountains would be struck by an enormous wave. The only land that would survive, in fact, would be between the Rockies and the Alleghenies and Catskills. The Midwest itself would be tilted toward the east. A new mountain range would spring up in the Mississippi valley. On the north and south would be new seas, formed from the Great Lakes and the Gulf of Mexico. What was left of the Western Hemisphere would be a much smaller island continent.

In the Eastern Hemisphere, Egypt would regain its fertility. France, England and Russia—all gone. On the other side of the world, the mythical continent of "Mu," sort of a Pacific Atlantis, would resurface.

Only Dr. Armstrong, his wife, and Marian knew of this prophecy. The destinies of millions were in their hands. So Dr. Armstrong did what he had to do. He issued a press release.

Hardly any newspaper ran it. A local newspaper did, and they reported it straight. Two other papers picked up the local account and ran it themselves.

Soon afterward, on Aug. 22, a UFO shaped like a half-moon was seen to hover, dart erratically in various directions, and bob up and down over Lake City. The same day, just outside Lake City, a couple of people saw a strange yellowish light in the sky. They happened to be members of the Civil Defense System's Ground Observer Corps, a long-defunct organization of civilians who supplemented the air detection network of the Air Defense Command. They called in news of the strange light, and two Air Force jet fighters were sent.

From the Associated Press account: "Two Air Force jet fighters, directed by ground observers, chased a yellowish light in the sky last night but reported that it blinked out when they started closing in on it. Air Force officers in the Minneapolis filter center said the blink-out of the light over the nearby community we are calling Lake City, Minn., was reported simultaneously at 11:48 p.m. last night by pilots and D.C. Scott, supervisor of the Center's ground observers in the Lake City area ... Ground observers said that when the planes gave up the chase the light reappeared and ascended rapidly in the night sky."

About 20 minutes later, a Ground Observer Corps post 20 miles to the northwest reported a glowing object which hovered, blinked twice, and then ascended out of sight.

The university researchers conveniently overlooked this.

Soon afterward, Marian received two visitors at her home in Lake City. One claimed to be a spaceman. They told her to keep quiet. Marian wasn't sure if they had been sent by Sananda or Lucifer, but she decided to not publicize the prophecy further. After those two came two more visitors, this time from the University of Minnesota. Marian remained pretty tight-lipped, but Daisy Armstrong happened to be around, and she filled them up with the prophecy. The Armstrongs were obviously more approachable. The university sociologists would retreat and regroup.

This time they sent two observers undercover to Collegeville, Dr. Armstrong's home turf. One failed to gain an entree. The other presented a made-up dream that was vaguely prophetic. She was embraced as a prodigal who had been sent by Sananda. Eventually four observers infiltrated a group which, at its largest, had numbered a hard-core dozen. Meetings followed; endless meetings during which Sananda wrote new teachings and refined old ones. The observers filled 65 one-hour reels of tape, which, transcribed, yielded 1,000 pages of typewritten text. No wonder Sananda preferred to dictate.

The sociologists ran into trouble Nov. 23 when one of the observers was asked to lead the meeting at Marian's. The observer hesitated; he mustn't "sway" the movement. He had to appear neutral. He told Marian that he was not "ready." Marian replied that he *was* ready. No further protests would be heard. "We all have to face our great responsibilities and take them," she said.

The following is from *When Prophecy Fails:*

"With nine expectant gazes transfixed on him, the observer fought for time: 'Let us meditate,' he ad-libbed, and bowed his head in silence. After a few minutes of silence, he asked Mrs. Keech to say a few words. She stated simply that the group had been called together for a special purpose; namely, the receipt of orders. She asked the observer if he had anything to add to that, but he had nothing, so the meeting returned to silent meditation as the tension mounted."

That lasted 20 minutes.

The group's attention shifted to Bertha Blasky, a clerk in her early 50s married to a firefighter, when she started panting and moaning.

She burbled over and over, "I got the words." Dr. Armstrong, disturbed, laid her out on the couch and took her pulse. Bertha's message continued, beginning with a recitation of the Ten Commandments. Then she declared that she was Sananda, speaking through Bertha.

"Oh, no, he can't mean me," sobbed Bertha, carrying on a dialogue with herself. Marian piped up with, "Oh, yes he does, Bertha. Yes, Bertha, he does mean you."

They all took a break to allow Bertha to recover. Then they went at it again. The important message from Sananda to his students, or "sibets," was thus:

"And the blessings of Sananda, on these precious, precious, precious, precious, precious, precious, precious, precious, precious, precious, precious, precious sibets ... and so it is, so be it, be it so, forever and ever, and ever, and ever, and ever, and ever, and ever, and ever, and ever, and ever, and ever, and ever."

That was at 10:30 p.m. Further intense concentration yielded nothing. After an hour, Bertha was ready to stop. But Marian said, "No, no, Bertha, you haven't gone the last mile yet." So they went on until 2 a.m. Finally Dr. Armstrong quietly told Marian that he thought Bertha was "off the beam," and that maybe they should let it go.

"It's a hard discipline, but you have to learn it," replied Marian. "I'm not going to take the responsibility for stepping in to stop her."

So they waited until 8 a.m. At that point, one of the members stalked off for home and bed. The meeting broke up.

At 11 the next night Bertha resumed her position at the center of the group, and this time she did not hesitate. She was forceful, dynamic. This leadership continued for the next several meetings, but on Dec. 3 Marian reasserted herself and received members one at a time in her cramped attic, where they received boarding instructions for the upcoming saucer voyage. Rule one: wear no metal. To do otherwise would be to risk serious burns. The university observer watched Dr. Armstrong rip the zipper out of his fly. Another member, Mark, "energetically removed the eyelets from a pair of his shoes." Frank wore a rope instead of a belt.

During all this, Marian also entertained a brand new sibet, keeping the regulars waiting for almost an hour and a half. Bertha fumed. Coincidentally, when the meeting finally began and Bertha went into trance, Sananda stuck it to Marian. Sananda, it seemed, had erred in some of his earlier lessons. He was going to set things right, and do it in plain language.

"I don't have to use any fancy words like 'thee' and 'thou' and 'shalt,'" said Sananda, the entity known in life as Jesus Christ. "We are talking cold turkey. You have had all the fancy words you need used on you before. There has been too much time wasted on this sort of stuff."

I actually rather like this new Sananda.

The first thing to go, under the new management, was vegetarianism. It had been rather strictly imposed before. (At the next day's meeting Bertha brought along a beef roast. The group tore into it—except Marian and the Armstrongs.) Smoking and coffee were still outlawed.

Finally, Bertha revealed to all the message that she had trembled to receive earlier in the week—the message that tore at her bosom, that caused her to disbelieve, that made her question her sanity; yet the peace of Sananda was infinite and his will, sure: Bertha was to give birth to the returned messiah!

Up to now, Bertha's sterility had been a pretty deep-seated concern of hers. But she was going to give birth—and not to any baby, but to Christ. As a matter of fact, right then, at 11 p.m., Bertha announced, "The baby will be born right now! I need help! Oh, doctor, help me! A bed must be prepared, I have pain. Something is happening in my abdominal area!"

Marian and Dr. Armstrong helped Bertha to the attic, of all places. According to the university observer, "after 10 or 15 minutes of groaning and writhing, she seemed to regain possession of herself and calm down."

This sort of stunned everybody, and no one knew what to think. Bertha, descending from the attic, said it was a mystery to her, as well, and that she sure hoped no one had thought she'd been making it up.

Then the thought occurred that maybe Sananda would be able to shed some light. Bertha tranced him up and, sure enough, he'd done it all as a little lesson for everyone, as a demonstration of his intention to "run this show" his own way. Also, Sananda said, it had been a joke. That way, the group wouldn't hold on to any preconceived ideas.

As a final miracle of the day, Sananda said, through Bertha, he would remove a skin blemish just beneath Bertha's right eye.

It didn't quite vanish. In fact, it didn't vanish at all.

Another lesson, said Sananda! This one a test of his sibets' honesty. Then he went on in an attempt to heal another sibet's long-standing fear of walking alone outdoors, which lasted an hour.

The sociologists noted, "the response of the various members of the group to Bertha's performance during these two (healing) sessions varied somewhat, but was, on the whole, accepting, almost as if they had been beaten into submission."

Dr. Armstrong, though, was ecstatic. With all the "pounding and pounding," he told his wife, "they're getting us ready for something big."

Long-term, of course—whatever Dr. Armstrong's something big was (as if the end of the world weren't enough)—in the short term he was fired from his job at a university clinic. He'd been converting, or attempting to convert, too many of his patient-students, and enough was enough. The media jumped on it, and whatever the reality of his belief system, Dr. Armstrong became the group's first martyr for it; many others would follow.

Bertha was next. Her husband said he was going to send her to a psychiatrist if she had not given up the group by the first of the year (doom was still set for Dec. 21). Her attendance at meetings was spotty from there on. Another member's husband refused to let his wife attend any more meetings at all.

There were new recruits, fortunately, mostly high school students. Also, by this time, the group included four university observers—almost half the total hard-core membership of 10. The University of Minnesota wasn't so much studying the group as subsidizing it, with bodies.

Another of the new members was Kurt Freund, a publisher of books on the occult and unexplained phenomena. This, of course, is a very honorable and intelligent thing to do. I salute him. And yet the university observers noted that at meetings he "yawned a great deal and slept part of the time." When asked by one of group what he was doing to prepare for the end, he said, "Nothing." When Marian sat in trance and wrote out personal teachings for him, "he was extremely inattentive—even leaving the room."

This attitude was not solely Freund's. The Dec. 14 meeting did not have a great deal of unity. The end of the world was a week away, but some of the staunchest members were waffling. Bertha, wan and tense, had been let out of her house for the evening but had only some hesitant communications to offer: "Accept no authority, not even the authority of the creator."

Additionally, the crush of media attention was creating stress for all. The early news release forecasting the end of the world was reaping belated interest, given Dr. Armstrong's dismissal. But Sananda had frequently told both Marian and Bertha—and others who attempted their own private seance/channeling sessions—that publicity was not to be sought. In fact, Sananda frequently reminded all to burn whatever notes they had. This made it increasingly difficult for university observers who had set out, more than anything else, to study the group's proselytizing; except for Armstrong's efforts, proselytizing was non-existent. Potential converts who showed up at the Keech home were either admitted or turned away based on the evidence of signs the newcomers may have received—dreams or other prophetic motivations. The merely curious were barred, and the media were spurned downright rudely. Years later, this stance would help ensure the former members' anonymity, so safely guarded by the writers of *When Prophecy Fails*, but makes it more difficult for later researchers to locate original source material in newspapers of the day.

Marian did break her silence, however, to accept an invitation to address a group of flying saucer buffs in a nearby city. Dr. Armstrong went as well, and offered hope of salvation to UFO fans when the end came.

"I'll say that all of you who are interested in saucers are in a special category," he said. "Now, you don't know that, but you are .... So don't be surprised within the next weeks and months ahead, regardless of where you happen to find yourself, if you find that you have an unusual experience in relation to spacemen or saucers or something of the kind. Because I think I can say to you—and it's no secret—that spacemen have said that they are here for a purpose and one of those purposes is to remove certain of their own people from the earth."

On Dec. 17, just days before the globe was scheduled to be sundered, Marian received a phone call. The group was practically living at her house by then, and they were fielding many calls from the press as well as from pranksters. This particular call came from a man who said he was Captain Video from outer space.

"Captain Video," of course, was a children's show of the period. Captain Video told Marian that a saucer would land in her backyard at 4 p.m. the next day, and she better be ready because avagadas don't wait for anybody.

They believed it. By noon the next day all five regular sibets had removed zippers, clasps, buttons, bobby pins and belt buckles, and the motley and loosely clothed group was ready. One member, Manya, still had her metal, as no one (even herself) was positive she was one of the chosen. Nevertheless, she quit her job just in case.

During the vigil waves of visitors came to Marian's home. As many as 15 were eventually admitted for coffee, talk, and a few answers. But no mention was made of the 4 o'clock saucer ride.

By 4, the visitors had been dismissed and the group gathered in the yard. By 5:30, they gave up and came inside to watch "Captain Video" on TV. Marian told everyone to watch for coded messages within the program—she was sure they would be there. But if there was a message, it was too cleverly encrypted, as no one noticed it.

That evening, Manya's boyfriend came to visit. He talked to people there. After a while he decided that his girlfriend might enjoy a Coke. In fact, it seemed like a very, very good idea to have a Coke. They would get a Coke, like, right now! They would go out for it, he said. But they'd be right back, very quickly.

He and Manya never returned.

No void is left unfilled, however. A 17-year-old boy turned up on Marian's doorstep. He said he had been sitting on a toilet, reading an article in the paper about the group, when a voice said to him, "It's true and you don't have to worry. You'll be picked up." He was admitted. About 25 others were met at the door, briefly entertained, and turned away.

At 11:30 p.m. one of the university observers left, returning an hour later to the news that a flying saucer was already en route to the backyard.

One of the members took her shoes and started to rip off the heels, for fear of the metal in the soles' nails. "I stopped him and said, 'Don't do that,'" said the observer later. "'Just get me a couple of pairs of wool socks and some bedroom slippers.' He did this and then pointed out that the buttons on my suit did have metal on them. I ripped the buttons off my coat. We got back outside again and Edna took me aside and said, 'What about your brassiere? It has metal clasps, doesn't it?' I went back in the house and took my brassiere off. The only metal on me was the fillings in my teeth, and I was afraid someone would mention those."

They waited until 3:20 a.m.

The next day, somewhat peeved, Sananda wrote, through Marian, "I have never been tardy; I have never kept you waiting; I have never disappointed you in anything." I think he just wanted to see the university researcher without her bra.

That night five boys briefly visited who claimed to be from Sananda's planet, Clarion. Dr. Armstrong was convinced that these indeed were "some of the boys from upstairs." There is no record, unfortunately, as to whether they wore metal. This was another test, Dr. Armstrong concluded. Two other members did not perceive what Dr. Armstrong read as their "brilliant minds." They said that they looked like "a bunch of kids trying to put on a front."

For her part, Marian wept with joy but also with fear. The continued "tests" were becoming too much for her.

On the morning of Dec. 20, Sananda sent the final, true instructions for the arrival of the saucer. It would come at midnight. Everyone relaxed. Some played games. All was well.

That evening, yet another check for metal was made. Also, all identification was to be left behind. The notes of Marian's that had not been destroyed were packed for travel.

At 11:15 Marian got a message to stand by. At 11:30, a member named Arthur remembered that his shoes had metal toecaps! There was a heated discussion, after which it was decided that he might simply take off the shoes immediately before boarding. At 11:35 one of the university observers remembered that he still had a zipper on his pants.

As reported in *When Prophecy Fails*, "This knowledge produced a near panic reaction. He was rushed into the bedroom where Dr. Armstrong, his hands trembling and his eyes darting to the clock every few seconds, slashed out the zipper with a razor blade and wrenched its clasps free with wire-cutters.

"By the time the operation was complete it was 11:50, too late to do more than sew up the rent with a few rough stitches. Midnight was almost at hand and everyone must be ready on the dot."

All waited in silence as the minutes ticked by. The clock ticked and ticked ... its hands passing 11:58 ... 11:59 ... midnight. Nothing! But there was another clock in the living room, and it showed only 11:56.

All waited in silence as the minutes ticked by. The clock ticked and ticked ... its hands passing 11:58 ... 11:59 ... midnight. Quoting Sananda, Marian shrieked, "And not a plan has gone astray!"

No one talked, no one moved. The phone rang, and reporters were told, "No comment."

Well, two hours later you would expect that the son of God would have caused at least a few earth tremors and sent down a scout ship. But he hadn't, so Marian went into a trance to get some answers. Sananda replied that he was a bit confused by her questions, and asked Marian for "something in writing" regarding his earlier statements. Finally Sananda revealed that there was another miracle he'd been busy preparing.

It was this: Marian's husband, asleep in the bedroom this whole time, would die and be resurrected!

Mr. Keech had gone to bed at 9. Three times, members went into the room to check—he yet lived. After 2, Sananda announced that the miracle had occurred. Marian's husband had died and been reborn. While he slept.

One of the teenage members went home—his mother had told him that if he hadn't returned by 2, she'd send the cops. The group broke for coffee. The hours passed—3 a.m., 4 a.m.—a university observer ducked outside to tape comments on a tape recorder—4:45, and Marian had Sananda's answer. The scheduled disaster had been averted — by the group!

"For from the mouth of death have ye been delivered and at no time has there been such a force loosed upon the Earth. Not since the beginning of time upon this Earth has there been such a force of Good and light as now floods this room, and that which floods this room now floods the entire earth."

This, Sananda said, was God's Christmas message to the Earth, and it could be shared—must be shared—with all of Earth's peoples.

The publisher, Kurt Freund, put on his hat and coat and walked out, apparently disappointed in the commercial viability of a book based on the message. The rest were jubilant. Reporters who had been scorned were rolled out of bed with the news. The Associated Press and United Press International news services were given the message. TV and radio, local and national—all were not only welcomed but sought, actively. Press releases were typed, interviews were taped over the phone. The world had been saved!

Marian's husband slept. I suppose being reborn takes it out of you.

By 8 a.m. the group settled down to watch national television and hear their Christmas message read back to them, over the air.

* * *

MINNEAPOLIS (ASSOCIATED PRESS)—A prophet of doom this morning said, "by intervention on the part of the God of earth, disaster has been stayed."

Mrs. Marian Keech, of 707 S. Cuyler Ave., Lake City, Minn., said she and her 13 disciples "had sat for the Father's message the night through and God has spoken. Not since the beginning of time upon this earth has there ...." (And so on.)

"Dr. Thomas Armstrong lost his job on the student health staff at the University of Minnesota by his acceptance of the prophecy. Armstrong, 44, said he would have "nothing specific" to forecast henceforth.

"I feel bigger things are in store for me. I'm not worried about a job," he said.

* * *

The group had survived. But the reason for its being had been lost.

The day the world was supposed to have ended, the group admitted any and everyone to Marian's home. The sudden and comprehensive availability of the group exhausted its newsworthiness almost immediately. It was a short, quick, funny story, quickly disposed of. There was one brief follow-up on Christmas Eve—aliens had promised to show up for Christmas carols in front of Marian's—and the group did meet and sing, and they did claim that aliens may possibly have attended, in disguise. More than 200 of the curious had been on hand.

"We couldn't see," Dr. Armstrong told one interviewer. Aliens in disguise, though? "I think—I think that's quite possible."

They had saved the world. But the world, and the world's problems, reasserted a claim for their attentions. The world was not kind.

Here's what happened next, for some:

Kurt—The publisher believed in the reality of flying saucers, but maintained a healthy skepticism. He was the first and most forthright in his departure.

Arthur—A high schooler, he maintained his belief in UFOs, but gave up the group's teachings.

Cleo and Bob—In the end, this couple was split. When the Christmas message was received, Bob said, "Yeah, I'll say it's interesting. The way it is around here your right hand doesn't know what your left hand is doing. Or if it does, it's a preconceived idea. I'm going to bed." Cleo continued to believe, and in May waited alone for another predicted saucer landing. Bob, reconsidering, said he was open to new orders from Sananda.

Clyde—This man had traveled 500 miles to be part of the group. He came out of the experience somewhat cautious, but still open to new messages.

Bertha—She continued her life, falling into doubt and depression over her role in events.

Mark—One of the youngest of the members, he maintained the group's remaining archives when Marian left Lake City.

Dr. Thomas Armstrong—He and his wife, Daisy, returned to Collegeville, where the doctor won a sanity hearing brought by his sister, who was concerned about his three children. She had meant the action as a precursor to a custody battle. The Armstrong family sold their house and left, supposedly for Virginia. They wrote to friends in Minneapolis that they continued to believe, and hoped to teach, and maybe even begin a lecture tour, based on what they had learned.

Marian—She continued to receive messages from Sananda, and mailed the new teachings to former members of the group. But she did so from hiding. The Lake City police, at the urging of parents whose children had been caught up in the group, told her husband that if she did not stop they would be forced to serve her a warrant for contributing to the delinquency of minors. She fled to a nearby town, then—alone—to Arizona, where she hoped to find a place in a center for what today we would call New Age theology.

* * *

In 1956 the University of Minnesota published *When Prophecy Fails,* a book which purportedly proves the hypothesis of its three authors that contradictory evidence only reaffirms faith.

That makes me smile, as this is shown to me every time I offer hard, concrete proof of UFO reality to supposedly scientific-minded folks who then throw up their hands and moan, "But it's impossible!" I have the contradictory evidence—their science is only faith.

To elaborate, I believe—well, rather, I know—that their science is actually faith, and that what they see as my faith is actually science: observe the phenomena—don't dismiss it. Learn as much as you can and then attempt to formulate a testable hypothesis that can explain it. Real science does not dismiss data that is inconvenient.

We are nowhere near a testable hypothesis. The so-called saucers and other phenomena could be from Clarion or who knows where. They could be from the son of God. There's as much proof one way as another. I'm open to suggestions. The data-gathering continues.

As for the Lake City group: I do not have a degree in sociology, but I wonder if it all wouldn't have failed much earlier without the apparent support of new believers—almost half of which were sent from the University of Minnesota. That in itself is bad science, and I think any results from the study are highly contaminated and suspect. In an atmosphere in which even celestial inactivity was interpreted by the true believers as significant, any pose of neutrality was in itself a dynamic part of Marian's evolving belief system. I would like to suggest that *When Prophecy Fails* became a classic in large part because it is so inadvertently entertaining. It's easy reading for undergrads.

Furthermore, I despise the researchers' refusal to incorporate into their book widely reported UFO sightings in the same time and place, thereby making the Lake City group look even more foolish.

As I pointed out earlier, it may be that part of what Marian shared was true—that she was in touch with something that is from somewhere else. I don't know if the somethings were aliens or ghosts, but I think they had, and have, a sense of humor. And I think they wanted *When Prophecy Fails* to be written.

You see, when the university observers finally parted from Marian, she gave them two messages from Sananda. The university people took those messages to be a reference to their network of contacts; they often knew when meetings of select members were to be held, etc., even though that information was held close.

In short, the university people knew more than they should have, and they believed that Marian read this as a suggestion that the sociologists were themselves from Clarion; she did not, of course, know until later that they were university sociologists.

I take Marian's final message to the researchers as just that Sananda's message to the researchers, urging them to take their notes and recordings and, yes, present it all to the citizens of the world, for better or worse, so that we might learn. We didn't, of course, in light of the Heaven's Gate tragedy. But you judge for yourself. Here is Mar-ian's final message to the members who were actually university infiltrators, as they left to prepare their book:

"So shall ye put your cards on the table and call an ace an ace and a spade a spade and ye shall also say who is who and what is what. And now do your duty as a brother."

I'll tell you, it sent a shiver up my spine as, older and somewhat wiser, I reread *When Prophecy Fails* for the first time since I'd been an undergrad. I think there was a truth here that the University of Minnesota completely missed.

Maybe I'm just a gullible flying saucer nut myself, but I hope I've finally been able to complete Sananda's work and do my duty as a brother, and call an ace an ace and a spade a spade and say who is who and what is what.

TRAIL OF THE VIKINGS

Why is Minnesota littered with medieval armament? For it is a fact that authenticated 12th century swords, axes and other battle gear have been found all over the state.

Here's a fairy tale. Parts of it are true. Once upon a time, long ago in a far-away land, there was a king named Magnus. He was a good king but not a good king. That is, he was good, but not at being a king. He ruled a mighty empire. Once a crook fled one of the king's territories. The crook went far away, over the waves. He found a new land. He came back and told everybody, and because he had discovered the new land, everyone forgave him. People went to the new land and prospered for many years.

One day, some of these pioneers vanished. Pffft! Just like that. Good King Magnus was sorry—very sorry. He sent men from his own bodyguards to search for the pioneers. They could not find them in the new land. They traveled farther and found an even newer land, but the pioneers weren't there, either. So the rescuers went home. Before they left the newest of the new lands, they chiseled an account of their journey onto a rock and left it ... in Kensington, Minn. It was 1362.

Columbus would not sail for the New World until 130 years later.

Minnesota was the inland landing spot for the first European discovers of America—according to a rock found near Kensington. In 1898 Olaf Ohman was clearing some land when he toppled a tree and found a stone tablet embraced in its roots. The stone had strange markings all over it. It was eventually carted to the University of Minnesota, where an imperfect translation was made. A copy of the ori ginal marks was then sent to the University of Oslo and other universities. Finally a comprehensive translation was made of what proved to be the ancient writing of Norway, "runes." It read:

"Eight Goths and 22 Norwegians on exploration voyage from Vinland (Newfoundland) through the west we had camp by two skerries (or boats—presumably the author means they landed and camped nearby) one day's voyage north from this stone we were and fished one day after we came home found 10 men red with blood and dead save from evil have 10 men by the sea to look after our ships 14 days voyages from this island year 1362."

If true, the inscription meant two things: that the Vikings had no punctuation! And that canny Norwegians had beat out Columbus by more than a century.

There's no harm in wanting your team to be first, of course, but from its earliest days Minnesotans have carried this to extremes. German writer Johann Georg Kohl, traveling through the territory in 1855, suggested that such an attitude might reflect the immigrants' predominantly Lutheran religion. Because in those days, Minnesota pioneers didn't settle for Vikings. They wanted to prove that the territory had been settled by more ancient explorers—remnants of the 10 lost tribes of Israel, who scattered around 720 B.C.

"It is very curious that I meet so many persons here still adhering to the belief in the Jewish descent of the Indians, not merely among the American clergy, but also among traders and agents," Kohl wrote. "Many cannot be persuaded out of this curious idea, though it seems to me to be more deeply-rooted in the Anglo-Saxon Protestants than the French Catholics. Perhaps this arises from the fact that the former employ themselves so much more in reading the Old Testament, the history of the Jews, and, above all, the final fate of the 10 lost tribes (of Israel).

"The latter they insist on finding here in America, and detect all sorts of Jewish customs among the Indians, which are, in truth, no more than the resemblances they bear to all other peoples that live in a similar nomadic state."

Ha! Let Kohl sneer. We have another theory, and more proof. It is not so wondrous that the lost tribes may somehow have made their way to Minnesota. After all, the area around Lamoille was the original Garden of Eden!

Yes, this was seriously suggested in the late 19th century by a Wisconsin clergyman, a Rev. Slyke, who just happened to live in the area. He pointed to the conjunction of the Trempealeau, Black, La Crosse and Mississippi rivers as meeting the Bible's description of Eden as a land where three smaller rivers meet a fourth, larger one. (Oh—and he said it didn't snow here then.) Slyke, being a good Wisconsinite, placed Eden in Wisconsin, but I see no reason why it could not have been across the river, in Minnesota (if it was even in this hemisphere).

With these sorts of stories being seriously tossed around, the legend suggested by the so-called Kensington Runestone was, by contrast, entirely reasonable. There was also some hard data on the other side of the Atlantic to bolster the runestone's truth. Most of it was uncovered by Hjalmar R. Holand, a Wisconsin scholar who first went to look at the Kensington Runestone in 1907, and who spent most of his life arguing in favor of its authenticity.

To understand why Vikings might have been in Minnesota in 1342, we have to go all the way back to the year 982. In that year Erik Thorwaldson was convicted of manslaughter in Iceland. Under the curious sentencing of the day, he retained his freedom, but anyone who wanted to kill him during the next three years could do so without fear of prosecution. Small wonder that he decided to take his family and voyage west—far west. He loaded up his ship, and several hundred miles distant discovered a country he named "Greenland" because it was, in his opinion, green.

Three years later he returned to Iceland with news of his discovery. Thorwaldson was now a hero, and there was a land rush. Greenland pioneers created an Eastern Settlement and a Western Settlement about 250 miles apart from each other. They flourished for 300 years. In 1261, Norway made Iceland and Greenland colonial possessions. At this time, the church was terribly powerful, of course, and as part of the new ownership, Greenland and Iceland bishops were appointed from Norway. As a sign of how out of touch Norway was with its possessions, however, when Greenland's Bishop Olaf died in 1280, his successor was not named until 1288. Similarly, when Bishop Arni died in 1349, the news didn't reach Norway until 1364.

In 1342 the Western Settlement was discovered to have vanished. Some sheep and cattle remained—they had turned wild. But the 90 farms had been abandoned, along with the population of 600 to 900. What happened to them has never been discovered, though there were some theories. Hjalmar Holand argued that they were "overwhelmed by the sneaking attacks of countless Eskimo," which is an image I enjoy tremendously—those countless, sneaking Eskimo. Others have suggested that the settlers had merely given up on the hard life and been absorbed by the native tribes, but Holand correctly points out that the residents of the Western Settlement were not newcomers toughing it out in the wilderness. They'd been there 300 years and had a cathedral. Maybe they were all killed—maybe they all fled, perhaps to a newer land, America.

Back in Europe, both Norway and Sweden were being ruled by King Magnus, who had already sent a crusade to Russia to convert its people to Roman Catholicism. When, in 1348, he learned of the disappearance of the Western Settlement, he saw it as a religious loss. Russia kept him busy until 1354, when he got enough money from the Pope to send an expedition to solve the mystery. It was to be commanded by the chief justice of one of his districts, Paul Knutson. The *Knorr*, a royal trading vessel, was to have been outfitted. Members of the king's own bodyguard would accompany Knutson, as well as anyone else Knutson might find helpful. In his orders, King Magnus wrote that the trip was to be taken "for the honor of God, and for the sake of our soul, and for the sake of our predecessors who in Greenland established Christianity and have maintained it until this time, and we will not let it perish in our days."

There is no actual evidence that the voyage was made, as skeptics have pointed out. But there's no evidence that it wasn't, and given the availability of personnel, funds and boat, plus the king's power and devotion to the church, I think it's reasonable to assume that Knutson did travel to Greenland.

What happened next is conjecture. Holand supposes that Knutson arrived in Greenland, found nothing, and decided to head west, in 1356, to a hypothetical land called Vinland, which today we would call Nova Scotia and Newfoundland. By 1360 Knutson and his crew could have searched as far as Hudson Bay. Perhaps they then decided to quit.

But before they did, they would send a scouting party even farther west, in light boats, to check for a possible passage to Norway—the idea being that the Thorwaldson party might have already landed in China, making the overland journey home shorter than a sea route.

It is just possible that the expedition sent a party through a tangled complex of waterways as far as Kensington, Minn., where they were attacked by Indians, carved the runestone, and finally headed back.

What did finally happen to the fleeing population of Greenland's Western Settlement? Hjalmar Holand believed that they, too, made it to Minnesota. The expedition would have found them if they'd looked just a little more. The Greenlanders merged with Native Americans, becoming the Mandan Indians.

The Mandans themselves are something of a puzzle. Captain Pierre La Verendrye, visiting a Mandan tribe in 1738, noted that their village was laid out European style, with blocks and streets. They lived inside a stockaded fort surrounded by a moat. As for the Mandans themselves, "This nation is mixed white and black," he wrote. "The women are fairly good-looking, especially the white, many with blond and fair hair." Their belief system was vaguely similar to Christianity.

All right, then, it is barely possible that a party as described by the Kensington Runestone could actually have been in the right place and time to carve it. Unfortunately, the best linguistic scholars have consistently found the stone's own language to be its worst fault. As early as 1899 Oluf Rygh, professor of Archaeology at the University of Oslo, said that its author "reveals himself to be a Swedish American who has become somewhat Americanized. Some English words have escaped him here and there. He has used several uncommon signs; where he has found them is uncertain, but in any event they speak against, not for, the authenticity of the inscription."

This criticism has since been echoed by countless other linguists.

Holand fought the linguistic battles for many years, attempting to explain why the stone's runes contained phrases too modern for its reported age, how inaccurate distances mentioned in it were actually correct if counted nautically, and so on. He looked at the stone's age and its weathering, and he even debated critics on the supposed diameter and age of the tree that had originally wrapped its roots around it.

A great deal has been written about whether or not the stone, if a hoax, was created by its alleged finder, Olaf Ohman. If so, the hoax was not a very successful one. There was a brief flurry of interest when

Olaf Ohman standing beside the
Kensington Runestone.

the stone was found in 1898, but Ohman did not exploit his opportunity. He did not take the stone to fairs and charge admission. He did not refuse to have it examined by the scholars who then called it a fraud. When they did so, he took the stone home and packed it away. When he finally turned it over to Hjalmar Holand, it was for only a few dollars, and he later said that he meant only to lend it to Holand, not sell it. (Today it can be viewed in the Kensington Runestone Museum in Minnesota's Alexandria.)

Still, the linguistic experts have spoken, and I am not overwhelmed by the "evidence" offered by the Kensington Runestone. I am impressed, however, by the fact that a lot of medieval armament has been found in Minnesota. That the pieces are authentic has been proven to my satisfaction. How the weapons got there remains a mystery. The stuff is rare enough in Europe, let alone here. I cannot imagine early immigrants dragging seven-century-old spears through Ellis Island, only to bury them in the prairie. Nor can I see hoaxers from this century going overseas to purchase such items at tremendous expense, just to bring them back as artifacts "found" in Minnesota. The many items could not have been made here; I believe the metallurgical tests are conclusive. But you judge for yourself. Here are some of the scattered implements found in the state and in neighboring vicinities along the supposed path of the Vikings:

OBJECT: FIRESTEEL

Description: A "U"-shaped piece of metal, with the arms bent in so far as to nearly form a squat "O"; the tips have curlicues.

Where found: On the bank of a former channel of the Red River, in Polk County, in a layer of charcoal and ashes.

Found by: Ole Jevning, while boring holes for fence posts in June 1871. "When I got about two feet down I heard something scrape against the auger and I pulled it up, thinking I had struck a stone."

Firesteels

Significance: Indians had had firesteels for some time, having traded for them with white settlers. This particular firesteel matches none used at the time, however. It is identical to Scandinavian firesteels of the 1300s.

Expert authentification: Eivind S. Engelstad, University Museum in Oslo: "The firesteel ... is of exactly the same type as the firesteels which have been found in Norwegian graves from the Viking age in great numbers."

OBJECT: CEREMONIAL HALBERD

Description: Sort of a long-handled axe with a spike on top. You still see halberds carried by guards in front of Buckingham Palace, and by the witch's minions in *The Wizard of Oz*.

Where found: On an eroding bank on the Dakota side of the Red River.

Found by: E. O. Estenson. "I saw the handle of the axes sticking out about 2 feet above the grassy surface of the bank."

Significance: The relic was not a relic of the fur trade.

Expert authentification: Charles E. Brown, of the State Historical Society of Wisconsin: "No implement is listed in any of the fur trade invoices that I have seen. In its expensive construction it is unlike all other trade articles. Moreover, the slender handle

Red River Halberd

makes it worthless as an axe for Indian use. It looks to me like an ancient Norse weapon."

Additional authentification: Sigurd Grieg, University Museum in Oslo: "Without a doubt ... from the period around 1500."

OBJECT: AXE

Republic Axe

Description: A heavy club-like blade, hooking down from an angular shaft.

Where found: In a stream near the present town of Republic, on the Viking's supposed path to Minnesota, in Michigan's upper peninsula.

Found by: A prospector, as he bent down to the stream to drink. He saw the axe and pulled it out. As he did so, the handle seemingly dissolved in his hand.

Significance: Wherever it is from, it is out of place. A twin to it was found in the Lillehammer Museum in Norway.

Expert authentification: Prof. W.C. Darrah, research curator of paleobotany, Botanical Museum of Harvard University: The remaining wood in the handle "might well have come from Norway or Northern Canada, but not from as far south as the Great Lakes. The wood as now preserved in the axehead is dense, mineralized, and obviously decomposed.... It is my opinion that this indicates a submergence in water for several hundred years."

OBJECT: AXE

Norway Lake Axe

Description: Similar to above.

Where found: On a peninsula projecting into the Norway Lake, in Kandiyohi County.

Found by: Ole Skaalerud, on a fishing expedition in the summer of 1908. "I picked it up and thought it must have been part of a seeding machine or some other machinery."

Significance: Identical artifacts not only can be found in Norway museums but also are featured in

13th century paintings of Norway's "ancient times."

Expert authentification: It was immediately recognized by the staff at several museums of Norway.

OBJECT: BATTLE-AXE

Description: An axe-head with the lower portion of the blade continuing down in a sharp curve toward the handle (broken in artifact).

Where found: Three miles southeast of Erdahl.

Found by: Julius Davidson, while pulling stumps on his farm in 1894. "Beneath one of these stumps he found this heavy axe of strange shape, the like of which he had never seen before," said Martha Davidson, his wife.

Erdahl Battle-Axe

Significance: This weapon was meant for use against armored opponents and has no use by Indians.

Expert authentification: Bengt Thordeman, assistant curator of the Historical Museum in Stockholm: The battle-axe "is in type practically identical with the St. Olaf's axe ... now in the National Historical Museum, dated 1468."

OBJECT: SWORD

Description: Ornamented with spirals and sunbeams, with a bronze handle and crossbar hilt.

Where found: Three miles west of Ulen, in Clay County.

Found by: Hans O. Hanson, while plowing in the spring of 1911.

Significance: The sword apparently had been in the possession of Indians, who hammered its tip off for use as a hunting knife; swords were of no use to Indians, though hunting knives were.

Expert authentification: The sword does vaguely resemble those created in a Romanesque style and carried by U.S. Army personnel in the early 19th century. Upon examination, however, the Smithsonian Institution stated that the sword was unfamiliar to

Ulen Sword

them. French or English trappers in settlement times would have carried rapiers, not Roman-style swords.

OBJECT: STEEL SPEARHEAD

Description: Long and narrow.

Where found: In a valley 40 miles east of Minnesota, across the Mississippi River, in Trempealeau County, Wis.

Found by: Nils Windjue, while clearing timber in the fall of 1899. "It was actually found by my adopted son, George Windjue, then about five years old, who was playing about and saw the spearhead turned up by the breaking plow."

Significance: The spearhead does not resemble those of English, German or French origin. It is characteristic, however, of Scandinavian spears of the Middle Ages.

Expert authentification: It was recognized by the staff of several museums of Norway as being a Viking-era spearhead.

Trempealeau Spearhead

OBJECT: CYLINDER WITH ATTACHED QUADRANGULAR SPIKE—USE UNKNOWN

Description: In shape the object resembles a lensless magnifying glass made from a single rude piece of iron.

Where found: On the east side of Lake Lakota, near La Grand.

Found by: Fred W. Kraftheger on his farm in 1938.

Significance: It is pointless to create for a hoax an object which is unrecognizable. One possible use for the implement is as a metal band around the handle of a pole, perhaps a pikestaff.

Expert authentification: Prof. R.A. Ragatz, chair of the Dept. of Chemical Engineering, University of Wisconsin: The metal dates to 1340 a.d. and was created in a wrought iron process not practiced in the U.S. since 1901. As a domestic hoax, it

Unknown

would have to have been created before that. "It is perfectly possible that this implement was made in medieval times."

OBJECT: SWORD

Description: Less ornamented than the sword on page 93, though the handle does have a zig-zag-patterned grip. There is no hilt.

Where found: Two miles west of Brooten, in Pope County, sometime between 1930 and 1940.

Found by: Andrew Stene, while plowing a spot in his field which had formerly been under a fence, and therefore unplowed.

Significance: Though more damaged, it is virtually identical to the Ulen sword described earlier.

Expert authentification: Prof. David J. Mack, chair of the Dept. of Metallurgical Engineering University of Wisconsin: "This structure consists of a high carbon wrought iron sword, a most unusual material which has not been made (to my knowledge) since the introduction of crucible steel two hundred years ago. This is a material which was used extensively by medieval armorers."

Brooten Sword

OBJECT: CEREMONIAL HALBERD

Description: Similar to halberd on page 91.

Where found: Near the edge of a grassy slough on a farm near Mt. Vernon, S.D., supposedly on the farthest edge of the Vikings' search, in September 1946.

Found by: Richard D. Knox.

Significance. Identical to the Red River halberd described on page 91.

Expert authentification: Prof. David J. Mack, of University of Wisconsin: "I feel it is probably an ancient halberd, certainly 150–200 years minimum. While I feel it is ancient, I would hesitate to say how it got there, although I believe (that the early Viking explanation is) absolutely correct."

Mount Vernon Halberd

Mora Axe

OBJECT: AXE

Description: Similar to the Erdahl axe.

Where found: Eight miles south of Mora, Kanabec County, in 1933.

Found by: William H. Williams while he was cutting corn.

Significance: Convinced of its authenticity, the Concordia College Museum acquired it.

Expert authentification: Dr. O.B. Overn, President of Concordia College and the School of Mines of the University of Minnesota: "It is wrought iron of a composition that has not been used in axes during the last two centuries."

* * *

There is one final problem with the Kensington stone and all of the associated weaponry found in Minnesota, and I doubt you'll ever guess it. In arguing that Minnesota was the ultimate destination for the discoverers of America—are the 14th century artifacts old *enough?*

The incredible irony is that the Kensington claimants were more right than they knew. They were arguing in favor of a Viking visit in 1362. At the time of the stone's discovery, in 1898, this was considered a fantastic, impossible story.

Then, in the 1960s, Yale University turned up a pre-Columbian map, the "earliest known and indisputable cartographic representation of any part of the Americas," proving that the legendary Leif Ericson had indeed voyaged to the New World—in 1117. And in Newfoundland, Canada, Norwegian scholars in 1961 excavated an entire Norse village that dated back to Ericson's day.

The Kensington party wasn't "impossibly" early to have discovered America; it was 245 years too late.

VIKING INDIANS?

The Mandans aren't the only Native Americans who have been described as European in appearance. There are at least two other tribes with those characteristics.

Wisconsin has the prehistoric Aztalan tribe, described by the later Woodland Indians as having hair like fire and eyes like ice. The Aztalan also had stockaded villages. One surviving female skeleton is 5 feet, 7 inches—tall for the time, especially for an Indian. Some of the men had faces like bears. The Ante-wandetton Indians who once lived near the Great Lakes said the visitors were "white people." The Menomonie recalled that the visitors had light skin. When presented with one of the visitors' copper artifacts recently excavated in the late 18th century, a Chippewa elder responded, "White man make long ago, way back."

The history of the Aztalan people goes back at least to 1000 B.C., far earlier than the supposed Norwegian expedition. Until 1198 B.C. the Aztalaners mined copper in Michigan's Upper Peninsula, retiring during the winter months to Lake Mills, Wisconsin. They were a wide-ranging tribe; Wisconsin Aztalan sites have yielded seashells from both the Atlantic and Pacific coasts. Around 900 A.D. they created a huge and complex city in southwest Illinois, at Cahokia.

The Melungeon tribe, in Tennessee, has members with tall builds, fair hair and blue eyes, and the tribe itself is unsure of its origin. Actually, to call it a tribe today is a bit inaccurate—until the middle of this century, to escape discrimination, the Melungeon found it beneficial to let outsiders assume they were of European origin. Many married outside the Melungeon community. Today there are only about 1,000 scattered Melungeon descendants, of mixed blood. The original Melungeon physical traits can be seen only in early photographs.

Ian Morphitt, writing in *The Fortean Times* magazine of unexplained phenomena, reports that the Cherokee called the Melungeon "moon eyes," because those features were less Asiatic than most Native Americans'. In 1673, British explorer James Needham described the Melungeon as "a white people which has long beards and whiskers and weares clothing." Some early settlers claimed that the Melun-geon spoke, or could speak, "broken Elizabethan English," though some of the names of individual Melungeons were strikingly similar to Portugese names. Some of the words in the Melungeon vocabulary, however, appear to be Turkish. For example, "Kentucky" comes from the Melun-geon for "dark and bloody ground," while the Turkish "kan tok" means "saturated with blood."

The name "Melungeon" was apparently given to them by French explorers who described the tribe as being a "melange" of mixed blood. The Melungeon called themselves "Portyghee."

CATTLE MUTILATIONS

Here is one of the farther-out conspiracy theories: The American government has long known that the flying saucers are real. After a crashed disc and its occupants were recovered near Roswell, N.M., President Harry Truman ordered the creation of a super-secret study group, code-named Majestic-12. This brain trust oversaw a subsequent meeting with the aliens, and cut a deal. Selections of alien technology would be delivered to the government if the visitors were allowed to abduct a small number of humans for brief experiments. The subjects would have no memory of these experiments.

Livestock was also to be taken. The reason for this, so the aliens said, was that they needed to harvest particular enzymes to aid their own dysfunctional digestive systems.

That is one of the wilder of the fringe theories attempting to explain the all-too-real cattle mutilations that have occurred in Minnesota and elsewhere. (There's another one, involving a secret Nazi moonbase established in the 1940s, but even I have my limits.)

Cattle mutilations are perhaps the oddest of unexplained phenomena. While other events—sightings of UFOs, ghosts and so on—are typically stories with no physical evidence, the mutilation of livestock provides grisly physical evidence in abundance, but with no accompanying narrative.

In the most classic of examples, one or more beef carcasses are found with organs removed with surgical precision. There are no signs of a death struggle, nor are there footprints or tire tracks nearby. Despite the profound mystery and lack of real clues in classic cattle mutilations, some observers have blamed UFOs, blood cults and even military intelligence agencies using black, unmarked helicopters.

"Cattle mutilations have been rather plenty around here," said Luane Hanson, a native of the town of Gully. In 1995 a 1,500-pound bull on a neighbor's farm was found dead. "The tail was cut out in a perfect circle and no blood was on the ground below." In fact, there were circular incisions all over the body. The body never hardened—it never underwent rigor mortis—even though the carcass lay around for a month. "It was still soft, like it had just died," said Hanson. All this is typical of mutilation reports.

"The veterinarian who came out to look at the dead bull also had spoke of some strange happenings," she said. "There were other mutilations in the Clearbrook area, not far from Gully. In one they saw an incision on the bull's leg. When they opened it up the bull's penis was inside. This sounds like something a cult would do, but there are too many strange coincidences"—coincidences having to do with UFOs (on page 105).

In Minnesota, reports of cattle mutilation come from many communities, including: Canby—Leonard Van Hyfte's farm, Nov. 5, 1973, and another unnamed farm northeast of town, Nov. 6, 1976; Ivanhoe—Paul Rolling's farm, May 1973; Kimball—Frank Schifelbein's farm, December 1974; Rock County—Charles Metzger's farm, Oct. 4, 1974; and the Carlos Avery Game Preserve, where numerous attacks were made on livestock from 1971 through 1977.

Typically, internal and external organs were missing. The incisions on the animals exhibited a precise surgical cutting. In one case reported by *Esquire* magazine, an unnamed Minnesota farmer found that the udder, sexual organs, and one ear of a cow had been taken. The udder had been removed by a diamond-shaped incision.

In many of the cases there has been evidence of extremely high heat at the excision sites. Though many animals are found in soft pastures and, in many cases, mud, there are no footprints, tracks, or marks to be found anywhere near the mutilated animals.

The interest of law enforcement agencies has waxed and waned over the years. Usually the phenomenon is taken most seriously at the local level, where the evidence is seen firsthand. One of the best and most recent official investigations occurred in Fyffe, Ala. In 1993 their police department released its report. The department had gathered as much national data as possible, hoping to find patterns that would have been unclear when considering only local mutilations. The report paints a chilling portrait of cattle mutilations nationally: 10,000 cases reported to—and documented by—law enforcement agencies in 49 states since 1967.

"To date no police agency has established a suspect or motive for these incidents of phantom surgery perpetrated on area livestock," the report states. There are no regionally distinct variations of the crime. "The organs and tissue taken are always the same: sex organs removed, tongue cut deep into the throat and removed; individual eyes and ears or sometimes both have been excised; the jaw stripped to the bone in a large oval cut and all tissue cut clean; rectums are cored out, almost like a stovepipe had been inserted and all the tissue and muscle has been pulled out." All of this has been accomplished on these thousands of animals with no evidence of blood present at the incision. In some cases the entire blood supply of the animal had been drained, yet without cardio-vascular collapse.

"Throughout the documented history of these cattle mutilations, no one has ever been charged or prosecuted with the crime. No one has ever been caught."

* * *

It has been suggested that there are many similarities between the alien-abduction phenomena and livestock mutilations. Both are loosely associated with UFO sightings. (Contrary to popular belief, when a human is abducted by what seems to be an alien, the victim merely finds him or herself in a room, usually without corners; rarely is an exterior view of a craft—UFO or otherwise—perceived.) Both phenomena also seem to center on the reproductive organs, and some human abductees do claim that the entities who have kidnapped them are doing the work on both humans and livestock to track environmental toxins.

If so, the kidnappers have been conducting their survey for centuries. In the 1970s cattle were the livestock most commonly mutilated in the U.S. But in the England of King Henry the VIII, in 1545, "the devilish act of cutting out the tongues of cattle" was common enough to earn its own statute. In the 19th century, horse "maimings" were unfortunately common in Great Britain; it was thought at the time that this was class warfare, merely an attack upon the property of the landed gentry. Arthur Conan Doyle, creator of Sherlock Holmes, even investigated one 1892 case and cleared a man falsely accused of being a member of a maiming cult.

The cult theory regained currency in 1974 when a professor at the University of Nebraska said that modern mutilations seemed to him to be "ritualistic" and perhaps the work of Satanic cults. Dr. Richard Thill, a professor of German (he also taught non-credit courses on witchcraft) told a reporter, "It could be someone setting up a fertility cult of some kind, or it could be someone putting you on. If they are putting you on, they are pretty sick."

There happened to be just such a man who might have been putting us on, and he may have been pretty sick. A. Kenneth Bankston, formerly of Minnesota, was serving time for bank robbery in the federal penitentiary at Leavenworth, Kan. He wrote to Kansas State Senator Ross Doyen that there was indeed such a cult. He had been a member, as had a friend of his, Dan Dugan, who was in a Texas prison. They would be happy to talk but feared for their safety once the Charles Manson-style "family" heard of their cooperation with authorities. The cult originally operated in Minnesota, he claimed, but moved to Texas when "family" members got in trouble with law enforcement. If Bankston and Dugan were transferred to safer facilities, they'd tell all.

A deal was cut and the secrets were revealed. Here's how they said the deeds were done: cult members brought large pieces of cardboard to the site. They put a piece on the ground, stepped onto it, and then put another piece ahead of them. Then they turned around and picked up the cardboard from which they'd just disembarked. That piece was placed ahead, becoming the next step on the path to blood. And so on. Presto! No tracks!

Meanwhile, the patient cattle supposedly chewed their collective cud as the stealthy cultists drew closer, closer, dancing from cardboard to cardboard. Undoubtedly they stayed put because they were laughing so hard.

Silly beef! Their laughter turned all too quickly to terror once the cultists came in range and shot the cattle with their trusty tranquilizer darts filled with angel dust. (In fact, traces of a different drug, nicotine sulfate, were found in the livers of some of the slain cattle.)

For a while a man who claimed to be a lecturer for the University of Minnesota claimed that the cattle had been shot (by UFOs, though, not cultists) in a way which "collapsed their blood structure with mercury." The supposed lecturer also claimed to be in regular contact with Bigfoot and was a regular visitor to the furry giants' homes.

One of the top civilian UFO research groups, the Aerial Phenomena Research Organization, noted, "Needless to say, his touted evidence connecting UFOs with dead cattle disappeared in the light of objective investigation."

But to return to the cult described by Bankston and Dugan: Once prone, the cattle were injected with heart stimulants, or amyl nitrate was held to the animals' noses—depending on the story. Either way, the cattle's hearts were induced to beat more quickly. Their neck arteries were punctured and the precious blood was caught in plastic bags. Once bled, they were ready for the bloodless surgery that was to follow.

When all was done, the cult members collected their sloshing bags of blood and bundles of organs and returned to the cardboard trail. Any stray marks left in snow were obliterated with blowtorches. Finally, round holes were punched into the ground to suggest UFO landing gear and throw researchers off.

Who were these clever devil worshippers? In 1975 Bankston and Dugan described the workings of their "Cult of Satan." It involved motorcyclists who resembled the Hell's Angels. But they hadn't acted alone. No. Stop a minute and think—what segment of society is the most evil, the most depraved, and would have the most to gain by worshipping Satan?

Yes! Millionaire stockbrokers. Bankston and Dugan said they had worked hand and glove with millionaire stockbrokers, all brothers under the cloak of Lucifer.

Together, the bikers and brokers worked secretly in 22 states. Their ultimate goal was larger, of course—much larger. News reporters, members of Congress and Minnesota Senator Hubert Hum-phrey were to be assassinated. There were plans, too, to steal a nuclear missile, steal plutonium and launch terrorist attacks.

As you can imagine, this news sort of caught people's attention, especially since the mutilations continued. In 1975 and '76 more than 1,500 cattle were killed and mutilated in 22 states. UFO researcher Jim

Marrs noted, "This would mean that the cultists had to locate, anesthetize, kill and butcher more than two cows each day. Counting travel time to each occurrence, the cultists would have had to spend every waking hour slaughtering cattle." The ranks of stockbrokers must have been decimated as executives across the Midwest called in sick and donned their cardboard snowshoes.

If you believe it all, that is. The scale of the operation argued against its reality, but assassination conspiracies were not to be taken lightly. Minnesota federal Judge Myles Lord ordered Bankston and Dugan north for questioning. The Bureau of Alcohol, Tobacco and Firearms joined the investigation.

Unfortunately for Bankston and Dugan, the man they fingered as the cult's Mr. Big turned out to have been in jail most of the time he was supposedly romping through Minnesota pastures. Other named leaders of the cult were hauled in, but they all passed lie detector tests relating to their alleged activities. In separate incidents, Bankston and Dugan briefly escaped jail, and authorities determined that such had been their intent all along. The two had made up the story after reading press accounts of the theorized cult.

There were real cults in other states, however. They had been investigated in Colorado. Carl Whiteside, chief of that state's Bureau of Investigation, said, "We could prove these groups existed, but we could never prove that they were involved in any criminal activities, including cattle mutilations. This doesn't mean they weren't responsible for a few of those animals. It just means we were never able to gather any evidence on it."

By 1979, the combined loss of livestock amounted to at least $2.5 million, as calculated by Senator Harrison Schmitt of New Mexico. UFOs, cults or whatever—he'd seen his constituency suffer long enough. He launched an investigation by the FBI. It quickly faltered.

Other governmental agencies were not ready to accept such prosaic answers. Back in Fyffe, Ala., an investigation of a mutilated Black Angus cow in January 1993 "revealed a flaky white material on the animal's right rib cage and on the ground 5 feet from the carcass," according to the police report. The material was placed in the empty wrapper of a cigarette pack and transported to the department.

While the flaky particles were being removed from the cigarette wrapper, the material came in contact with the brass tip of a ball-point pen. "Within one second of contact with the brass, the material melted

THE UFO COINCIDENCE

While UFOs are often suggested as being responsible for cattle mutilations, they are not always seen near mutilation sights.

In other places, such as the town of Gully, both mutilations and UFO sightings take place with alarming frequency. Luane Hanson, age 20, not only has been witness to cattle mutilations, she has had three UFO encounters:

"I have grown up in a rather desolate farm community. My parents live approximately 15 miles from the closest town, Gully, which has a population of approximately 150. My first encounter was in the early part of December, maybe four years ago [1993].

"I would guess that it was approximately 8 p.m. My parents and I were driving home after getting a Christmas tree. We were driving by Thief River Falls, down a 'less traveled' road. The road turns to gravel approximately one mile from the church (located northwest from home). We just passed the church when we saw a light in the air. It appeared to be a light far off in the distance. I thought it was an airplane at first.

"But suddenly that light shot at a very rapid speed at a 45-degree angle. I said to my parents, 'It's going to crash.' It appeared to be crashing at a very rapid rate of speed. It looked like it went into a grove of trees. It seemed so bizarre that something would move that fast at that angle going straight into the ground. My parents saw what I did. It seemed like only a moment.

"The second time I had an encounter was when I was driving home from work. It was 2 or 3 a.m. in mid-July of 1996. I was approximately 18 miles from home. This sighting was only four or five miles from the River Road Casino.

"I had driven past the casino, and two other vehicles were in front of me. I was listening to the radio just watching the road. All of a sudden I looked up and there was this huge object probably the size of a trailer house. All of a sudden this thing was above the road. It looked like it was only 150 or 200 feet in the air. It approached the highway from the north and slowly passed over the highway to the south. It crossed over the highway only a quarter or half mile ahead of me.

"I looked up and saw the bottom. It had multi-colored lights—blue, red, yellow, etc. They kind of made the shape of a pyramid. The thing passed directly over the highway. The funny thing was that I did not hear a sound from the huge object as it crossed the highway. I was deathly scared. I didn't want to look at the thing. I just got this helpless and scared feeling in my stomach. I didn't know what to do. I was all a-lone. I really wished at the time that the thing would just disappear. I was seriously considering turning around and going to the casino. But the thing looked like it was going to make a loop and return towards the highway, towards the casino. The other option was to cruise home as fast as possible. So I accelerated up to around 90 m.p.h. I passed one car, which was going around 75 to 80 m.p.h., and the other one was long gone (it had sped away even faster). The other two vehicles had been only driving 60 m.p.h. before I saw the thing.

"I got home and locked myself in the bathroom for an hour before I came out. It's not a good feeling at all!

"The third time was the fall of 1996, when I was driving home from a night class at the college. I remember it was November. I looked over, and above the trees a bluish light appeared. It looked like it may have been following the tree tops; I truly don't know what it was. I couldn't hear any sound.

"I am not some crazy person who is saying this for publicity. So, if you don't want to believe it—don't!"

into an almost clear liquid. To reduce the risk of this happening to the remaining material, the rest was shaken out into a jar, where it remained unaffected. This white, flaky material was then air expressed to a molecular biologist at a leading eastern university for analysis.

"After two tests, the scientist determined that the substance was composed of aluminum, titanium, oxygen and silicon in significant amounts. He stated that the amount of titanium was larger than he would ever expect to see in any substance and that there was no way this combination of elements could ever occur in nature."

Federal agencies may be doing nothing about the mutilations, but some rather odd people with government ties are.

In 1994 Terry and Gwen Sherman purchased a ranch in the Uintah Basin, in Utah. They didn't know it at the time, but the ranch had a history of strange happenings. After two years, during which the family experienced a bizarre series of UFO sightings and cattle mutilations, they were ready to quit. An unlikely purchaser was found in 1996—Robert Bigelow. And if you thought the opening of this chapter was loopy, just hold on.

Robert Bigelow is a Las Vegas businessman. He has a long-standing interest in UFO research, and in 1995 alone he is said to have donated $1 million to the three largest UFO investigative groups, the Mutual UFO Network (MUFON), the Fund for UFO Research, and the Center for UFO Study (CUFOS). According to Philip Klass, the top UFO debunker in the country, in 1995 Bigelow teamed with former U.S. Army Col. John Alexander. Alexander is the former head of the Los Alamos Nonlethal Weapons research program.

Alexander already had a history of professional interest in UFOs. In February 1987, when Alexander was at the Pentagon's Defense Intelligence Agency, he convened an interagency working group to study UFOs on an ongoing basis. The UFO Working Group, at least initially, included one Army and three Air Force generals, Defense Intelligence Agency scientists, an Army colonel, three officials from the National Security Agency, a supervisor from the CIA's domestic intelligence division and a technical team from the CIA's Science and Technology Directorate. The work of the group, and even its existence, were secret; while researching a book on the Walker spy family, former *New York Times* reporter and Pulitzer Prize nominee Howard Blum was led to the UFO Working Group by a National Security Agency official. Blum published his findings about the group in his book *Out There*.

Among other things, the UFO Working Group investigated the entire community of Elmwood, Wis., about 40 miles from St. Paul. The town had a high number of UFO sightings, including an incident in which a police officer apparently received a fatal dose of radiation. The Elmwood investigative team was drawn from the CIA Domestic Collection Division.*

Alexander has since joined Bigelow's National Institute of Discovery Science (NIDS) in Las Vegas. The institute is said to be involved in ESP research and theoretical UFO engineering. NIDS describes itself in a prospectus as "a newly formed, privately funded research organization. It focuses on scientific exploration that emphasizes emerging, novel, and sometimes unconventional observations and theories. In its programs, NIDS rigorously employs accepted scientific methods and maintains the highest ethical and quality standards. Because NIDS is a new institution, it is too soon to determine exactly what specific projects will be undertaken. However, the Institute is concentrating on exploring fundamental research on issues concerning the nature and evolution of life and consciousness in the universe, and their modes of interaction."

This fundamental research on the nature and evolution of life would seem to include—you guessed it—cattle mutilations. NIDS now operates the Sherman ranch in Utah. The property boasts an observation tower and a staff that includes a pair of scientists and a veterinarian. Needless to say, the land has since been fenced. Gates are locked and "Keep Out" signs are posted, but NIDS still has a friendly side: it mailed 1,200 letters to area ranchers asking for their cooperation in reporting missing or mutilated animals.

"Bigelow and Alexander will not discuss the doings on the ranch," reported the magazine *Spirit: Rocky Mountain Southwest,* in the fall of 1997.

As part of the deal, the Sherman family signed a non-disclosure agreement barring them from discussing their experiences while in residence at the ranch.

I'd almost prefer a blood cult.

---

* A full account of the UFO Working Group's investigation of Elmwood may be found in my earlier book, *The W-Files: True Reports of Wisconsin's Unexplained Phenomena.*

FAIRIES AND SUNDOGS

N ot all unexplained phenomena are horrific. Some are funny, and some are even pleasant—almost magical. These phenomena include fairies, black snow, extra suns and raining corn.

It really did rain corn on April 30, 1967, over the town of Crystal. These sorts of things are called "falls" in the lexicon of unexplained phenomena. All sorts of things come down, from fish to frogs to spider webs. Why this is, isn't really known, though scientists suggest the probable explanation of tornadoes and waterspouts sweeping up objects and transporting them many miles before they fall. The weather can be strange—but it is seldom inexplicable.

But what, for example, are we to make of this report, which appeared in the *New York Times* in 1889?

"Aitkin, Minn., April 3—A peculiar phenomena [sic] occurred here yesterday. At 4:45 o'clock it became so dark that lights were necessary in business houses and the air was filled with snow that was as black and dirty as though it had been trampled into the earth. Six ounces of snow and 1/4 ounce of dirt and sand were found in the bottom of a dish. The dirt is very fine, something like emery, and contains particles that have a metallic lustre. This dirty snow fell to a depth of half an inch. The atmosphere at the time presented a pe-culiarly greenish tinge. There was a little wind blowing at the time from the northwest, though there seemed to be considerable wind higher in the air. Solid chunks of ice and sand are reported to have been picked up in various places."

If that were not enough, what if you looked up and saw eight suns? It happened, in Sauk Centre on Dec. 30, 1880. Ice crystals in the air commonly cause halos around the sun or moon, and the phenomenon of the "sun dog," or mock sun, while rarer, is similarly explained. But what happened in Sauk Centre is truly bizarre—though perhaps not supernatural.

From the *Scientific American:*

"The sky was clear, save that the air was full of floating frost crystals that gave a leaden aspect to the heavens around. The sun ... was surrounded by a double halo, both very perfect and distinct in outline.

"To the right and left of the sun and on the rim of the first halo were very bright parhelia, or mock suns. Passing through the sun and these mock suns and around the whole dome of the heavens, seemingly, at about 20 degrees from the horizon, was a great circle of light. This had the appearance of the large ring of Saturn—very bright and about 1/4 of a degree in width. Again about 15 degrees from the rim of the outer or second halo and in the path of this circle of light, were other parhelia on either side of the sun; and on the opposite side of it from the sun was another or third parhelion. This circle was very brilliant, describing a diameter of about 100 degrees.

"Intersecting this bright circle, at the points of the two parhelia, passed a somewhat less brilliant ring of light in the form of an ellipse, with its longest diameter some 130 degrees and the short one 80 degrees. At the northern end of the ellipse were three parhelia."

In all, eight parhelia, or mock suns; there are some dim Midwestern days when I'd settle for two.

Finally, I leave you with stories of impish sprites: fairies. While we don't seem to see them in these modern times, once they were not uncommon.

In 1831 the Rev. Peter Jones came to the territory that would later become Minnesota to visit the Chippewa, or Ojibwa, Indians, for the "amelioration of their condition consequent on their conversion to Christianity."

He was born in Canada and reared until the age of 16 by his mother, an Ojibwa herself. His Welsh father got him baptized and converted to Methodism. Peter Jones sincerely enjoyed Christianity and worked to share it. And he sincerely enjoyed the Indian way of life, but saw it polluted by the influence of European adventurers. Oddly, to modern observers, he seemed to see Christianity as an inclusive bridge between the European and Indian philosophies. He worked as a missionary, but also as an amateur anthropologist.

He committed to paper, among other stories, legends of the Mamagwasewug, the hidden or covered beings—fairies.

"Many old Indians affirm that they have both seen and talked with them," he wrote. "They say that they are about two or three feet in height, walk erect, and have the human form, but that their faces are covered up with short hair."

European settlers encountered the fairies, too. From Jones' notes:

"In the year 1824, a Scotch family, residing on the banks of the River St. Clair, were visited by some strange invisible agencies. The first attack was made on their poultry, which were taken as if with fits, and soon died; then the cattle, pigs, and horses were seized in the same manner, and died. After this the house was attacked, and stones and pieces of lead were thrown against the windows, breaking them and entering the house. The pots and kettles were then moved from their places without anyone being near them. An attempt was next made to burn the house. Live coals of fire were found tied up in tow and rags in different parts of the chambers, which were extinguished as soon as discovered; but eventually the house was burned down.

"While these occurrences were taking place, a vigilant watch was kept up by the family and neighbors, who flocked in to witness these strange scenes; but no clue could be discovered as to the cause.

"It was finally declared to be the work of witchcraft. Accordingly, a celebrated witch doctor, by the name of Troyer, residing near Niagara Falls, was sent for, to expel all the witches and wizards from the premmises. Being on a missionary tour to the Walpool Island Indians at the time these incidents were going on, I went to the enchanted house, and preached the ever-blessed Gospel; but the mischievous spirits were all very quiet, so that I saw nothing out of the common order of things.

"But the Rev. R. Phelps was more fortunate, for he told me that when he visited the family, and attempted to preach, they kept throwing in small stones and bits of lead, one of which struck his body. This he picked up, and he showed it to me.

"On my return from the St. Clair, I met an old man who, from his appearance, wearing a long flowing beard, I judged must be the witch doctor. I therefore asked him if he were Mr. Troyer. He replied, 'I am.'

"He then positively stated that he knew the whole affair was witchcraft, and that he would soon make a finish of the witches. I was afterwards informed that he began to expel them by firing off guns loaded with silver bullets, which he stated were the only kind of weapons which could take effect upon a witch. Whilst he was in the midst of his maneuvering, the neighboring magistrate, hearing of what was going on, issued a warrant to take him into custody. The great doctor, being apprised, quickly made his escape to his own quiet home. This ended the whole affair of the supposed witches and fairies.

"In conversation with a noted pow-wow chief, Pashegeeghegwaskum of Walpool Island, I asked him what he thought about these strange occurrences among the white people. He replied, 'O, I know all about it. The place on which the white man's house now stands was the former residence of the Mamagwasewug, or fairies. Our forefathers used to see them on the bank of the river. When the white man came I pitched his wigwam on the spot where they lived, they removed back to the poplar grove, where they have been living for several years. Last spring this white man went and cleared and burnt this grove, and the fairies have again been obliged to remove; their patience and forbearance were now exhausted; they felt indignant at such treatment, and were venting their vengeance at the white man by destroying his property.'

"The old chief uttered these words as if he fully believed in the existence of these imaginary beings, and in their power to harm those who dared disturb their habitations."

The Rev. Jones told another story of the fairies, very similar to that of the Irish leprechaun. An Indian caught a woman fairy in his wigwam one night, releasing her only after she promised that he would receive good luck if he did so. The fairy was released, and "success attended him."

Jones noted that the fairies love guns, are fond of shooting, and that he was puzzled as to how they must acquire firearms unless they steal them. The fairies love red cloth, and cloth printed in wild patterns. If you meet one and provide the fairy with a piece of such cloth, no matter how small, you're sure to receive "long life or success in hunting."

The Rev. Jones was careful to call the fairies "imaginary," but he also sounds as if he's not entirely unconvinced, and perhaps even wistful. "In all my travels through the wilderness I have never been favored with a visit from these invisible fairies."

I do not know if the Mamagwasewug are real. I hope they are. I like anyone who has a sense of wonder so childlike as to be excited by a piece of bright cloth.

I would like to think that we would still notice the Mamagwasewug today, but a few thrown stones or bits of lead in today's fast and loud cities would hardly be noticed. I hope we have not built too often on their settlements, and—if we have—that they have been able to safely remove to other poplar groves.

PLACE-NAME INDEX

Unless otherwise indicated,
cities and villages named are within Minnesota.

Agassiz, British Columbia, xv
Aitkin, 37, 109
Alabama, 52
Alamogordo, N.M., 61
Albert Lea, 28, 37
Alberta, Canada, xi
Alexandria, 90
Anoka, 22-23, 28, 37
Anoka County, 10
Argentina, 61
Arizona, 24, 82
Arkansas, 27
Asia, 17
Augusta, Wis. 23
Austin, 37

Bagley, 37
Baraboo, Wis., 29, 30
Barron County, Wis., 51
Beaver Lake, 38
Belgium, 6
Bemidji, 1, 2
Bigelow, 31, 38
Biwabik, 38
Blaine, 38
Boston, Mass., xiv
Breckenridge, 31, 38
British Columbia, xv
Brooten, 95
Brookston, 38
Burnsville, 38
Byron, 38

California, 6, 7, 24, 25, 27
Campo Rico, Puerto Rico, 24

Canada, xi, xii
Canby, 100
Carver County, 38
Cedar, 38
Chanhassen, 40
Chatfield, 16
Chattanooga, Tenn., 23
Chicago, Ill., xiv, xv, 25, 27, 29, 33, 36
Chile, 64
China, xi
Chisago City, 38
Chisolm, 38
Clay County, 93
Clearbrook, 100
Cloquet, 38
Collegeville, 63, 69
Colorado, 41, 104
Comstock, 38
Cook, 38
Coon Rapids, 22, 38
Connecticut, xiv
Cotton, 18
Cottonwood, 38-39
Crookston, 15
Crystal, 39, 109
Cumberland, Wis., 51
Cyrus. 39

Dayton, Ohio, 52
Detroit Lakes, 39
Dilworth, 39
District of Columbia, xiv, xv, 26, 53
Dresbach, 16
Duluth, 18, 28, 31, 39-40, 41
Eagle Bend, 40

Eau Claire County, Wis., 23
Eden Prairie, 40
Egypt, 72
Elbow Lake, 31, 40
Elmo, 32
El Paso, Texas, 61
Elmwood, Wis., 108
England, 101
Englewood Cliffs, N.J., xiv'
Erdahl, 93, 96
Erskine, 40
Essig, 31, 40
Excelsior, 28, 31, 40
Exeter, N.H., x

Fairfax, 40
Fall Creek, Wis., 23
Faribault, 40
Farmington, 40
Farwell, 40
Fergus Falls, 31, 40
Fillmore County, 16
Finland, 40-41, 61
Floodwood, 17, 41
Florida, 24
Forest Lake, 41
Fort Ripley, 41
France, 14, 26, 72
Freeborn County, 37
Fyffe, Ala., 101, 104

Garvin, 41
Glenwood, 41
Golden Valley, 41
Graceville, 41, 42
Grand Marais, 42
Great Britain, xv, 36, 102
Great Lakes, 13, 72, 97
Greenland, 87-88
Greenwich, Conn., xiv
Gully, 100, 105-106

Hastings, 31, 42
Hastings, Nebr., 27

Hector, 31, 42
Henderson, xii
Herman, 42
Hibbing, 42
Hollywood, Calif., 6
Hong Kong, 3
Houston County, 16

Iceland, 87
llinois, xiii, xiv, xv, 25, 27, 29
Indiana, 13
International Falls, 42
Invale, Nebr. 27
Iowa, 27, 43, 46
Island Lake, 18
Israel, 86
Ivanhoe, 100
Iwo Jima, 59

Japan, 53
Jonesville, 31, 42
Juarez, Mexico, 61

Kanabec County, 96
Kandiyohi County, 92
Kansas, 27, 43, 102
Kensington, xiv, 85, 89
Keokuk, Iowa, 27
Kimball, 100
Kinbrae, 42
Kingston, 42

La Crescent, 16, 46
Lac Qui Parle Lake, 42
La Grand, 94
Lake City, 62-84
Lake Coronis, 16
Lake Crystal, 28, 42
Lake Elmo, 42
Lake Kimo, 31-32
Lake Lakota, 94
Lake Lillian, 31, 42
Lake Mills, Wis., 97
Lake Minnetonka, 28, 42

Lake Pepin, 63
Lake Sara, 41
Lake Superior, xv, 50
Lake Winona, 50
Lamoille, 87
LaSalle, 42
Las Cruces, N.M., 61
Las Vegas, Nev., x, 107, 108
Los Alamos, N.M., 107
Leavenworth, Kan., 102
Lengby, 43
Lindstrom, 43
Little Falls, 9, 43
Little Fork, 43
London, England, xv, 4
Long Lake, 18
Long Prairie, 9-10, 43
Luverne, 43
Lyle, 43

Madison, Wis., xi, xiii, 29
Madison Lake, 31, 43
Mankato, 31, 43
Maryland, xv
Massachusetts, xiv, 8, 24
McGregor, 43
Medford, 43
Medina, 44
Mexico, 24
Michigan, xiii, 97
Michigan City, Ind., 13-14
Middle River, 44
Midwest (U.S.), 13, 37, 72, 104
Mille Lacs (Lake), 44
Milwaukee, Wis., 3
Minneapolis, 25, 27, 28, 33, 37, 44-
    46, 53, 54, 55©58, 60, 72, 81, 82
Minnesota, northern, 13
Minnesota, southeast, 51
Minnesota-Iowa border, 43
Minnesota-Wisconsin border, 51
Minnetonka, 27, 31, 46
Mississippi River, 14, 16, 87
Missouri, 27, 45

Mojave Desert, 67
Montgomery, 31, 46
Montgomery, Ala., 52, 64
Moorhead, 46
Moose Island Lakes, 16
Mora, 96
Motley, 46
Mound, 46
Mount Everest, Nepal, 1
Mount Vernon, S.D., 95
Movil Lake, 46
Mud Lake, 46

Nebraska, 25, 27, 33, 102
Nepal, xi, 1
Nevada, x
New Brighton, 46
New Hampshire, x
New Jersey, xiv, 3, 24
New London, 46
New Mexico, 37, 56, 104
Newfolden, 46
Newfoundland, 86, 88, 96
Newport, 46
New Scandia, 46
New Ulm, 31, 46
New York, xiv, xv, 24, 29, 61
Niagra Falls, 61
North Dakota, 47
Norway, 88, 89, 92, 94
Norway Lake, 92
Norwood, 31, 46
Nova Scotia, 88

Ohio, 52, 55
Omaha, Nebr., 25, 33
Oregon, xii
Oslo, Norway, 86, 89, 91, 92
Owatonna, 46

Philadelphia, Penn., 61
Pine City, 16
Pine River, 46
Polk County, 91

Pope County, 95
Preston, 31, 47
Puerto Rico, 24

Quebec, Canada, xii

Rainy Lake, 47
Rainy River, 16
Rancho Santa Fe, Calif., 62
Reading, 47
Red River, 91, 95
Regal, 47
Republic, Mich., 92
Riderwood, Md., xv
Robinsdale, 48
Rochester, 13, 47
Rock County, 100
Rock Creek, 47
Roseau, 47
Roseville, 47
Roswell, N.M., 99
Royalton, 31, 48
Russia, xi, 72, 88

Sacramento, Calif., 25, 26-27
Sacred Heart, 47
St. Anthony, 47
St. Clair River, 111-112
St. Cloud, 47
St. George, 47-48
St. Louis Park, 48
St. Paul, xiv, xv, 26, 33, 48-49,
    60-61, 108
St. Peter, 49
San Francisco, Calif., 27
San Jose, Calif., 27
Sauk Centre, 110
Scandia, 49
Seattle, Wash., 53, 64
Shafer, 49
Shevlin, 49
Shorewood, 49
Siberia, 3, 17

Sibley County, 49
Sleepy Eye, 31, 49
Starbuck, 49
Stewart, 49
Stewartville, 49
Stillwater, 31, 49-50
Stockholm, Sweden, 93
Sunrise, 50
Sweden, 88
Sweetwater, Fla., 24
Syracuse, N.Y., 61

Tasmania, 23
Taylors Falls, 28, 50
Tennessee, 23, 98
Texas, 24, 27, 102
Thief River Falls, 50, 105
Todd County, 10
Togo, 50
Topeka, Kan., 27
Totem Town, 50, 61
Tower, 17
Trempealeau County, Wis., 94
Trempealeau River, Wis., 87
Two Harbors, 50

Ulen, 93
Utah, 107, 108

Vermont, xii
Villard, 50
Virginia, 82
Virginia, Minn. 31, 50

Walker, 50
Warren, 16
Waseca, 28, 50
Washington, D.C., xiv, xv, 26, 53
Waukesha, Wis., 23
West Battle Lake, 50
West Orange, N.J., 61
White Bear Lake, 50
Windom, 31, 50
Winona, 3, 4, 7, 31, 50

Winsted, 51
Wisconsin, xi, xii, xiii, 3, 14, 23, 24,
    27, 29-30, 47, 50, 53,87, 91, 94,
    95, 97, 108
Woodside Township, 51
Wyoming (Minn.), 50

Young America, 31, 51

MORE BOOKS
FROM WISCONSIN TRAILS

Walking Tours of Wisconsin's Historic Towns
Elizabeth McBride, Lucy Rhodes, Anita Matcha

Paddling Northern Wisconsin
Mike Svob

W Is for Wisconsin (child's book)
Dori Hillestad Butler / Illustrated by Eileen Dawson

Portrait of the Past
A Photographic Journey Through Wisconsin 1865-1920
Howard Mead, Jill Dean and Susan Smith

The W-Files
Jay Rath

Great Wisconsin Restaurants
Dennis Getto

The Wisconsin Traveler's Companion
A Guide to Country Sights
Jerry Apps / Illustrated by Julie Sutter-Blair

Great Wisconsin Walks
Wm. Chad McGrath

Great Weekend Adventures
The Editors of Wisconsin Trails

County Parks of Wisconsin
Jeannette & Chet Bell

Best Canoe Trails of Southern Wisconsin
Michael E. Duncanson

Best Wisconsin Bike Trips
Phil Van Valkenberg

Barns of Wisconsin
Jerry Apps

Wisconsin The Story of the Badger State
Norman K. Risjord

WISCONSIN TRAILS
P.O. Box 5650, Madison, WI 53705
(800) 236-8088 E-mail: info@wistrails.com